I0889612

TORRY

David Herd & Ian Stewart

TORRY

The Life and Career of

TORRY GILLICK

a Footballing Great

pitch

First published by Pitch Publishing, 2024

Pitch Publishing
9 Donnington Park,
85 Birdham Road,
Chichester,
West Sussex,
PO20 7AJ
www.pitchpublishing.co.uk
info@pitchpublishing.co.uk

© 2024, David Herd and Ian Stewart

Every effort has been made to trace the copyright. Any oversight will be rectified in future editions at the earliest opportunity by the publisher.

All rights reserved. No part of this book may be reproduced, sold or utilised in any form or transmitted in any form or by any means, electronic or mechanical, including photocopying, recording or by any information storage and retrieval system, without prior permission in writing from the Publisher.

A CIP catalogue record is available for this book from the British Library.

ISBN 978 1 80150 902 2

Typesetting and origination by Pitch Publishing

Printed and bound by Thomson Press, India

Contents

This book is dedicated to the memory of

Molly and Torry.

Together forever.

ACKNOWLEDGEMENTS

THIS BOOK would not have been possible without the support of the Gillick family. Their enthusiasm for the project and their great sense of pride in Torry's achievements shone through in all our many conversations. We hope that they feel as much pride in reading the finished publication.

We would also like to thank Everton FC historian David France, and Rob Sawyer of the Everton Heritage Society for providing invaluable information on Torry's career with another historic football club. It is obvious that the name Torry Gillick is held in great affection at Goodison as well as at Ibrox.

Thanks also go to John Henderson, the historian of Airdrie FC, and Albert Moffat, the Petershill FC historian. Without their great help, unearthing the details on Torry's career at these two clubs would not have been possible.

Finally, our heartfelt gratitude to Peter Waddell and John Gilligan for providing the forewords for the book. It meant so much to include a member of the Waddell family; the names Waddell and Gillick are forever interlinked in any discussion on the greatest right-wing partnership in Rangers history. John is a man who helped save the club in 2015 and will always be admired by the Rangers support.

FOREWORD

by Peter Waddell,
son of Rangers legend Willie Waddell

I WAS pleased to be asked by Ian and David to contribute to the foreword of their book about of one of my late father's best friends during his playing days at Ibrox.

My father was enormously proud of his time at Ibrox; firstly, of course, as a player, then manager, general manager and director. I know myself, my older brother, Ronnie, and sister, Ailsa, were equally proud of him. His greatest and enduring legacy is the magnificent stadium we all sit in today and we are privileged that we still attend every home game at Ibrox as guests of the club.

Rangers was, essentially, my father's life. Since his debut at the age of 17 against Arsenal, when he scored the winning goal, until the day he died in 1992 at the age of 71, he always put Rangers' best interests before anything else in life. He enjoyed a successful eight years as Kilmarnock manager, resigning after winning the league championship in 1965 but he was delighted to accept the board's invitation to return to Ibrox as manager in December 1969.

Under his management in 1972, the team won their only European trophy, the Cup Winners' Cup. The role of manager back then was much different to what you see in football today. Not only did my father deal with playing matters, he was responsible for the entire running of the club. He spent as much time with non-playing staff, like the late Lizzie Love, as he did with the players. Then, of course, there was the seismic impact of the disaster in 1971 and the demands upon him became greater still. It was that tragedy that made him determined to rebuild the stadium and ensure it could never happen again.

I was born in 1955, just as his long Rangers career had come to an end as a player and the great Iron Curtain side of the post-war years was breaking up. By then, the legendary William Struth, commonly known as Bill, had been replaced as manager by Scot Symon.

It was during the war years that he struck up his lifelong friendship with Torry. He obviously knew of Torry, as his reputation as a player and a character went before him, and it is ironic that he joined Rangers just after Torry had left for Everton. However, when Torry returned in the early war years, they struck up an immediate bond as the principal creators in the Rangers forward line.

My father also told me that that great side was full of characters and dyed-in-the-wool Bluenoses. There was no greater character than Torry. My father recalled there was never a dull moment when he was about and there was always a laugh to be had. Not only was Torry a character but a highly talented and effective footballer.

Family holidays in those days, like most folk's, tended to be spent in Scotland. One of my own personal memories of my father and Torry involved us going to visit him in the north of Scotland while he was on a salmon fishing holiday. I will not divulge the detail here, as it is covered within the pages of Ian and David's book, but it summed up the character of Torry and what life was like around him. 'Never a dull moment' is the phrase I often heard.

As the years passed, they grew a little apart due to the jobs they had and, inevitably, the time they spent together dwindled. Father gravitated more towards Willie Thornton, of course, and Ian McColl when he returned to the club in the late 1960s.

I do vividly remember, though, that when Torry passed away in December 1971, my father penned an emotional and heartfelt tribute to his great friend in the *Rangers News*. It summed up just how much my father valued their years together and how proud they both were to have pulled on the blue jersey together.

I hope you like this story of a great footballer and a man I enjoyed meeting.

FOREWORD

by John Gilligan,
former director of Rangers FC

WHEN I was born in the Springburn area of Glasgow in 1952, there were many uncertainties in life for everyone. One thing that was never in doubt for me was the football team I would support. My father and uncles were passionate Rangers fans and I was always destined to follow in their footsteps.

My first match at Ibrox Stadium was perhaps an unusual one. I was taken along to a reserve team cup tie against Celtic at the age of ten. By coincidence, in the forward line for Rangers were two other Springburn boys who would both go on to make a name for themselves in the royal blue. Jim Forrest and Alex Willoughby were cousins and they lined up alongside another future star in wee Willie Henderson. Rangers won 2-1 and I discovered the joy of being there to see my team defeat their greatest rivals, albeit not in a major competition. I would, of course, see countless battles between the old foes in the years ahead. I remember the wins better than the defeats!

The first big occasion I was allowed to attend was the visit of the great Real Madrid team to the stadium in the European Cup in 1963. I remember the massive crowd and how I was left down at the white wall at the front of the terracing while the adults stood further back to get a better view. That was definitely something that would never happen these days with seated stands and a society where we keep our eyes on our children at all times. It was an incredible experience; the sheer noise and the excitement whenever Rangers went forward against the most glamourous team in world football. Sadly, it ended in disappointment when, after Rangers had had the better of the match, the masters of Madrid broke away in the last few minutes and the great winger Gento set up the famous Hungarian star Puskás to score the only goal. It was only a few years ago that I at last got some revenge for that night when Real finally returned to Ibrox to play a friendly to celebrate 150 years of Rangers. This time, I got the perfect view in our wonderful modern stadium as we won 2-1.

The crowd that night in 1963 exceeded 80,000 and, at the time, I couldn't imagine there could be any bigger attendances. But, of course, the man who is the subject of this book played in front of many even bigger crowds. What an experience it must have been to be in amongst 140,000 at Hampden and even more amazing to play in such an atmosphere. And Torry Gillick didn't just play in these huge occasions, he scored goals in them.

In the years that followed that 1963 match, I became a regular supporter, home and away. Until I was old enough to travel to the matches without adult supervision, it was usually by car with the occasional bigger game via the Bishopbriggs supporters' bus. It left from a pub called the Crow and, to this day, I keep in touch with a few of the regulars. I saw some unforgettable games, such as that special day at Easter Road in 1975 when Colin Stein scored to give us our first league title in 11 long years and halted Celtic's run of championship wins at nine.

But even that wasn't my all-time highlight. In 1972, I spent the massive sum of £60 to get over to Barcelona to watch Rangers play Moscow Dynamo in the final of the European Cup Winners' Cup. When the final whistle sounded and we had won 3-2, it was a feeling money couldn't buy. I've seen two more European finals since then, although unfortunately neither was able to match the team of 1972, who remain my biggest heroes. I loved Stein up front and worshipped the wonderful Alex MacDonald in midfield. But if I had to pick just one Rangers hero, it would be the captain, John Greig. An absolute rock for Rangers in good times and in bad. It's amazing to think I now sit just a few seats away from him at Ibrox.

By the early 1980s, a tough time to be a Rangers fan, I had bought my first season ticket, which got me into the new Copland Road stand or the enclosure under the main stand. I can't remember the exact price, but it was around £50. That meant a whole season of Ibrox games cost me less than getting to Barcelona a decade earlier. There have been so many other great days in my Rangers lifetime. I was there when Walter Smith's team won our nine-in-a-row at

Tannadice, the goal scored by the brilliant Brian Laudrup. Then there were two of the wildest celebrations I can remember. First, in 2002, when Peter Lovenkrands scored a Scottish Cup Final winner in the last minute to defeat Celtic. I never thought that would be beaten for an eruption of joy, but then along came 'Helicopter Sunday' three years later. The celebrations that followed the news reaching Easter Road of Celtic conceding in the last minute of the league season sounded like there had been an explosion!

As all these unforgettable occasions were happening, my career with Scottish Brewers was going well. With McEwan's Lager sponsoring Rangers, my position in the company allowed me access into the inner circle at the club as a hospitality host, giving me the chance to make so many friends and create many more memories. The late Sandy Jardine also worked for Scottish Brewers and our friendship is a particularly special memory. By the time I became managing director of Tennent's, Sandy was back working for the club and our paths crossed regularly.

Sandy wasn't the only Rangers great I was fortunate enough to know well. I was part of Walter Smith's testimonial committee and chaired the committee which organised the benefit match for midfield hero Ian Ferguson. Fergie is one of a small band of players who has ten league championship medals that were all won with Rangers.

My business knowledge, combined with my well-known affection for Rangers, meant that I became active in another way. Rangers, under chairman David Murray, had accumulated significant debts and I helped in the foundation of the Rangers Supporters Trust. The trust aimed to ease these financial worries by looking to buy shares, attract fan investment and have a say in the running of the club. Unfortunately, our attempts to help weren't encouraged and the club ended up in the hands of owners who did not represent the best interests of Rangers and their supporters. We all know the result of this in 2012 and the misery of the next few years.

In 2015, Dave King, Paul Murray and myself were successful in buying enough shares to take control of the club and to put it back in safe hands. It is a matter of massive pride for me that I was involved in this, especially when Dave and other board members would refer to me as 'always a fan first'. I saw myself as the fan representative during the takeover and serving the club on the board until 2017 was the experience of a lifetime. I was heavily involved in the recruitment of manager Mark Warburton and his assistant, David Weir, and I still think those guys are underappreciated for the job they did under difficult circumstances. In fact, they probably achieved too much too quickly and I was as guilty as anyone of getting carried away after we beat Celtic in the Scottish Cup semi-final at Hampden.

My time on the board is behind me now, although I'm still made very welcome at Ibrox, and if I'm not in my season ticket seat, I'm in the directors' box. I remain in close touch with John Bennett, Douglas Park and other directors and will never forget what they have done for our club. My season ticket in the main stand is a prized possession and always will be. My dad, back in his day, never needed a season ticket. It was a totally different culture back in those times; supporters simply paid at the gate. His earliest hero was the great captain Davie Meiklejohn, a man who won even more league titles than Ian Ferguson. But the team he spoke about most was the one who won many trophies and played in front of those huge crowds in the years just after the Second World War.

There were 11 names he would reel off: Brown, Young, Shaw, McColl, Woodburn, Cox, Waddell, Gillick, Thornton, Duncanson, Caskie.

Like so many Bluenoses of his generation, that was HIS team. And in that team, he was in no doubt who was the great entertainer and the man who had the skill and vision to do the unexpected and turn a draw into a win. That was Torry Gillick. In my time, there have been a relatively small number of these maverick players, the ones who defy convention and who have magic in their boots that others can only dream about. I saw Baxter, Gascoigne and Cooper, and all three were exactly the kind of player every great team needs. Massively talented stars who the crowd wanted to see and who were both a part of the team but also individuals who could go it alone when the mood took them. Gillick belongs in their company.

I have heard so many Gillick stories, both on and off the field. His love of greyhounds. His dislike of the Ibrox dress code that Bill Struth insisted upon. How he would only put on his bowler hat as he turned into Copland Road to try to fool his manager into thinking he wore it the whole journey. His reluctance to chase after a pass that was too far off target for him to reach. And, of course, his fabulous skills that were a major reason why that Rangers team won so many trophies and are still talked about to this day. He also had an unforgettable clash with Moscow Dynamo!

I recently visited the Rangers Museum, which is a fantastic place with so many items from the club's past. One special display for me is the Hall of Fame wall. In the early 2000s, I attended many of the Hall of Fame award dinners where some great players were announced as being inducted into the elite band of the greatest Rangers players. Sometimes a player was announced who had played in the distant past and was no longer here to pick up his award. When the name of Torry Gillick was inducted, I remember the ovation he got, despite having passed away decades earlier. Very few in the audience probably ever saw him play. That tells you everything about how special his name is and always will be. His picture is now in the museum and his story is being told in this book.

It is my privilege to write these opening words as his amazing story is now told. I hope you enjoy reading about him.

CHAPTER 1

THE EARLY YEARS

GARTNESS IS a small village on the edge of the Lanarkshire town of Airdrie. In the 19th century, it was part of a heavily industrialised area, with iron works and coal mines providing employment for the local population. It is, perhaps, a village not particularly known to the majority of the people of Scotland, especially since the demise of these old industries. But Gartness has a claim to fame in the world of Scottish football, as it was the birthplace of a footballer who carved out a unique career in the blue of Rangers, Everton and Scotland. His name was Torrance Gillick, but he would become known throughout the football world as Torry.

His father, Lawrence, was born in 1891 in Moffat Mills near Airdrie, the youngest child in a family of 12. Coal mining was a hugely important industry in the area, with young Lawrence joining several family members and school friends in becoming a miner in the local pit. He would meet and then marry a local girl, Isabella Sinclair Ferguson, on 2 June 1911. The happy couple then settled in Gartness, where they remained for the rest of their days.

The couple welcomed their first child, a daughter they named Annie, in 1913. Then, as Britain was enduring the hardship and the horrors of the Great War, their next child came along. This time it was a boy, who they named Torrance, a name that had also been given to one of the newborn's many uncles and went back generations in the Gillick family. He arrived into the world on 19 May 1916, blissfully unaware of the desperate times the country was enduring.

Lawrence was in a protected profession, the country desperately needing coal to provide the power for homes and industry and to underpin the war effort. Having already started a family prior to the 1914 declaration of war, Lawrence would not have been enlisted, although many young fathers in non-protected professions were accepted as volunteers.

Young Torrance would end up as the middle child, with Lawrence and Isabella's second daughter, Kate, being born just after the war ended to complete their loving and close-knit family. With a mother he adored, and two sisters at home, Torry would be well looked after by the Gillick ladies as he grew up.

Torry was a child with a keen sense of adventure and one who, from an early age, showed great natural ability at football. The sport was the nation's favourite getaway from the hard times following the conflict, with massive crowds attending the biggest matches in Scotland and most young boys dreaming of stardom wearing the colours of their favourite team. At Moffat Mills Primary School, young Torry shared that distant dream and, unlike the vast majority of other lads, he was showing the natural talent to perhaps make those dreams a reality.

He would be seen kicking a ball with his friends for as long as his mother allowed him to stay out and he quickly became the first player chosen for team games in the streets or the playground. As he progressed to secondary school at Airdrie High, he was quickly the star player – not just for the school itself, but for the local district. A player with dazzling ball control, a consummate ability to beat a defender and a deadly accurate shot, Torry racked up the goals and the accolades.

By 1928, at the age of 12, he had been instrumental in helping his school win the local schools championship for their age group. By 13, he had been snapped up by the crack local side Clarkston Juveniles and he was quickly playing in age groups far beyond his tender years. Around this time, father Lawrence had left the mines to start work in one of the local paper mills, a job that allowed him to support his family and didn't involve the dangers of underground life. Torry was now very much hoping his future life would be in a very different world again – that of professional football.

However, he wasn't the only promising footballer in the family. In fact, there were many in the Gillick clan who thought his cousin, Jim Gillick, was even more talented. Torry and Jim were very close, possibly due to their shared love of the game. But Jim was a painfully shy boy and he found it difficult to get changed and bathed before and after a match in a communal dressing room setting. He was known to even attempt to wear his football kit under his clothes and simply put his shirt, jacket and trousers back over the top of his muddy strip rather than undress in front of his team-mates. This shyness and a reluctance to mix with other young men would eventually drive Jim away from playing the game, despite cousin Torry's attempts to change his mind. Maybe Scottish football would have celebrated two stars named Gillick had circumstances been different.

Torry wasn't particularly academic; his ambitions from early on were aimed at the football pitch rather than educational achievements. Away from football, he also developed a love of fishing from an early age. His father and his uncle, Bob, were both keen anglers in the local waters and Torry would often be seen with them casting a line if he wasn't leaving defenders in his wake with a ball at his feet. Both sports would be a passion for the rest of his life.

Bob, who was two years older than Lawrence, was the man who showed Torry how to make and cast a fly, a skill that he was to hone over the following decades. Their favourite spot in later years was in Callander, many miles north from when their love of fishing together started. But no matter how effective his own flies would be, Torry kept hold of those Bob had made him all those years ago, as they seemed to have that extra magic that was needed to outwit the fish.

On leaving school, Torry's heart wasn't in any job that might come along. His goals were attracting attention in the football community and it looked only a matter of time before a club would persuade the rising star to sign on the dotted line. In 1932, that club finally came calling, and 16-year-old Torry Gillick was on his way to stardom.

CHAPTER 2

THE JUNIOR STAR

IN 1932, junior football in Scotland had a far more prominent place within the game than today. This was long before most senior clubs decided to create their own academies where the most talented youngsters would be recruited from an early age and developed into future stars. There were no B teams full of promising teenagers. This meant many of the most sought-after youth players would begin the next stage of their football education in junior football, with those who excelled being scouted and snapped up by senior clubs.

The Rangers team of the time had some star names who had been recruited from the junior ranks. Legendary names such as club captain Davie Meiklejohn and long-serving defender Dougie Gray were spotted and recruited from Maryhill Juniors in Glasgow and Aberdeen Mugiemoss. And 1932 was the year in which a precocious young centre-forward called Sam English set the Rangers club record for league goals that still stands to this day, just a few years after being signed from Yoker Athletic of Clydebank. There would be other great stars of Ibrox who would join from junior football in the years to come: the likes of George Young from Kirkintilloch Rob Roy and Eric Caldow from Muirkirk.

The junior game in Scotland was split into regional leagues, with a multitude of local cup competitions on the calendar alongside the ultimate prize of the Scottish Junior Cup, a nationwide knockout competition which attracted some huge crowds. In Glasgow, there were many junior clubs, some of which were regular contenders for honours. Petershill FC played in the Springburn area in the north of the city and in 1932/33 they started the season in great style in the Western Division of the Central League. The Peasy, as they were known, had assembled their best side since their glory years between 1911 and 1918 when they had won the Scottish Junior Cup three times and the Glasgow Junior Cup once.

They started the season with five straight wins, centre-forward George Fulton starring with seven goals including all four in a 4-3 win over Duntocher Hibs. By the end of October, The Peasy were locked in a battle at the top of the table with Renfrew, with Fulton by now boasting 18 goals for the season in league and cups. They then suffered what appeared to be a mortal blow to their title dreams. St Johnstone of the First Division, managed by former Rangers skipper Tommy Muirhead, had been watching the progress of Fulton and decided to take him north to Muirton Park after the player had claimed two more four-goal hauls in cup wins over Strathclyde and St Anthony's. He would go on to score many goals for the Perth club, including strikes in wins over both halves of the Old Firm in 1933. His departure left Petershill with a huge gap to fill and left their title challenge hanging in the balance.

Petershill had other goalscorers in their team, particularly inside-forwards Jimmy Connor and Archie Mason. However, the loss of Fulton unbalanced their attack and a miserable November saw them lose in the league to both Duntocher Hibs and Benburb, as well as crash out of the West of Scotland Cup in the first round to Shawfield. In early December, they decided a replacement centre-forward was a must and their sights turned towards Airdrie and the teenage sensation of schools football in the area. Petershill became the new footballing home for Torry Gillick.

As debut appearances go, the first sight of 16-year-old Gillick in a Petershill shirt could hardly have been more spectacular. On Saturday, 10 December 1932, the teenager played centre-forward at Petershill Park for the first time. The opposition were another Glasgow team, St Roch's, who were the first club of another famous Scottish football star of the time, the great Celtic goalscorer Jimmy McGrory. A hard-fought encounter saw Gillick the match-winning hero, netting all three Petershill goals in a 3-2 victory. His second appearance seven days later continued his dream start with his new club, scoring both goals as title rivals Rob Roy were defeated 2-0. Two Petershill games, five Petershill goals – and all scored by the sensational Gillick. The following weekend, the Petershill fans finally saw someone else hit the net for their team against Arthurlie, a penalty scored by James McFadyen. But the points were banked thanks to a winning goal smashed home by their new hero. It was Christmas Eve and the Gillick star had been born.

The year ended with a first disappointment at his new club for Gillick, an unlucky single-goal defeat in the Scottish Junior Cup away at Bonnyrigg Rose. But with six goals in his first four games, Torry was already on the radar of bigger clubs and many at Petershill Park were wondering how long they could hold on to their new goalscoring machine. By the end of February 1933, the club were already resigned to this being Gillick's only season in Petershill colours, with an ever-growing number of senior scouts watching on as the goals continued to flow. When he grabbed a double in a vital 3-1 win over championship hopefuls Yoker, Gillick had rattled home nine goals in just four February fixtures, the highlight being five in a Glasgow Junior Cup quarter-final demolition of Vale of Clyde.

As the business end of the season approached, the goals kept coming at a remarkable frequency. When Gillick scored a crucial winner in a 2-1 Central League Cup victory at Cambuslang Rangers on 15 April 1933, he had scored in 16 out of 18 matches, having scored the previous day in another cup match against Glasgow Perthshire. Keeping Torry Gillick off the scoresheet was now the hardest task in junior football and it was no coincidence that Petershill's only league defeat so far in 1933 was the one match in which he failed to beat the opposition goalkeeper, a 3-1 defeat to Pollok in mid-March. It was now common knowledge among the fans that Rangers were keeping a close eye on their talisman, with inside opinion being that the player would see Ibrox as his ideal destination.

The Western Division of the Central League was reaching a tense climax. Petershill held a two-point advantage over second-placed Renfrew with the teams meeting at Renfrew's Western Park in the final fixture. Perhaps the Petershill approach was too cautious in a match where a draw would win the title or maybe home advantage gave Renfrew a crucial edge. Whatever the reason, a 16th Torry Gillick league goal made little difference as The Peasy were swept aside 5-2, meaning a one-off championship decider between the teams was needed. Incredibly, it was scheduled for the following day, with Firhill chosen as the neutral venue.

Renfrew must have gone into the match as favourites after heavily defeating their opponents just 24 hours earlier, and a dispirited Petershill lost the decider 2-0, with Gillick given few chances to shine in front of a crowd of 10,000. However, this wouldn't be the end of the Western Division drama. The Renfrew team in both matches had featured inside-forward Tom Cumming, whose recent signing should have rendered him ineligible for league matches. Petershill appealed to the Central League that his inclusion broke the rules of the competition and that they should be awarded the title. The appeal committee agreed and Renfrew were deducted the two points they had won in the 5-2 match. It meant Petershill, with 43 points from 30 matches, were declared Western Division champions and they would take on Strathclyde Glencairn at the beginning of the following season to decide who were the Central League champions.

Petershill would win that match 3-1 on 5 August 1933, but by then Torry Gillick was no longer their centre-forward. He scored his 30th and last Petershill goal in a 1-0 win over Yoker on May 26 in the Kirkwood Shield quarter-final and made a forgettable last appearance for The Peasy in a crushing defeat at the hands of Pollok in the final of the tournament the following week. His 30 goals in half a season meant the now 17-year-old Gillick had already outgrown the junior game. His destination was no surprise – he was to become Torry Gillick of Rangers.

Years later, Gillick, recalling the day the legendary Bill Struth welcomed him to Ibrox, reflected: 'I shall always remember the day he signed me. He gave me the impression that I wasn't signing for a football club, but that I had entered into the most magnificent football organisation in the world. I didn't know it then, but he was right.' On 24 June 1933, Petershill FC received a transfer fee of £75, while the player was paid a signing-on fee of £20 and promised £3 per week in wages. In the years to come, it would be hard to argue that this was not one of the best value deals the club would ever do.

CHAPTER 3

WELCOME TO IBROX

IN THE summer of 1933, Gillick joined a Rangers team who were back at the summit of Scottish football after regaining their league title from Motherwell to claim a sixth championship in seven seasons. The teenager may have been a sensation at junior level, but he now faced incredible competition to get a starting place at Ibrox, where Bill Struth had assembled a squad packed with talent.

One position that was still up for grabs was on the left wing, the position which had been the property for over a decade of the legendary Alan Morton. The 'Wee Blue Devil' had retired earlier in the year and Struth had not yet settled on a long-term successor to a player many regarded as irreplaceable. The 1933/34 season started with Willie Nicholson on the left of the Rangers attack, with veteran centre-forward Jimmy Fleming occasionally being utilised in a wider position instead. Gillick started life at Ibrox in the reserves, where he played alongside several notable names from the club's future and its past.

In late September, Rangers faced a hectic series of fixtures. On Saturday, the 23rd, they beat Dundee at Ibrox before a 1-1 draw two days later in an Old Firm Glasgow Cup semi-final. The Wednesday saw the team travel to London to play Arsenal in a glamour friendly at Highbury, with Fleming scoring twice. The team then returned to Glasgow for another derby match at Firhill against Partick Thistle. After a gruelling week, manager Struth rang the changes in his forward line. One of these changes was to move Fleming infield to centre-forward to replace the injured Jimmy Smith and to give a debut to Torry Gillick on the left wing. His inside-left partner was another recent arrival trying to make the breakthrough at the club, Irishman Alex Stevenson. In years to come, they would be team-mates for many years, but this was the only time they played together in the Rangers first team.

There were 20,000 inside Firhill on Saturday, 30 September 1933 to witness the first competitive first-team appearance of a Rangers player who would go on to play almost 400 more. And it was a match to remember, with Gillick coming out on the winning side in a seven-goal thriller. The youngster didn't score in the 4-3 win, but his clever use of the ball impressed everyone watching. Impressive it might have been, but this was still too early in Gillick's career to expect him to be a regular starter. He was back in the reserves after his taste of the big-time, although it wouldn't be too long before another opportunity arose – and with it the chance of a first medal.

The Glasgow Cup tournament was due to be completed in mid-October, but the replayed semi-final against Celtic couldn't be fitted into the schedule until the Wednesday before the final. Rangers had a centre-forward crisis, with inside-forward James Marshall utilised as an emergency central striker for the Old Firm clash at Ibrox. A late Alex Stevenson goal won the match 2-1, but Marshall looked ill at ease in his temporary role and, with both Fleming and Smith still unavailable for the final against Clyde, manager Struth decided to give young Gillick a chance in the position he had been such a sensation in at Petershill.

Hampden was the venue on Saturday, 14 October, with an attendance of just under 24,000 watching as Gillick was tasked with leading the line for the holders and helping bring the season's first trophy to Ibrox. It took 40 minutes for Rangers to break the deadlock and it was Gillick's invention that created the goal. Instead of looking to score when a looping cross came into the box, he cleverly headed the ball back across goal to wrongfoot the Clyde defence and there was right-winger Bobby Main running in to slot the ball home. From then on, the favourites never looked threatened and a second-half strike by the great Bob McPhail gave the scoreline a more realistic look.

Gillick, at just 17, had his first winner's medal as a Rangers player and the press were impressed with the exciting young forward. The *Glasgow Herald* report of the match singled him out for praise, stating Gillick 'gave quite a good display' and that 'his ball control and passing were up to standard; more will be heard of him'. Much more would be heard of him, of course, but not a lot of it in the 1933/34 season.

Rangers won the clean sweep of honours, adding the league title, the Scottish Cup and the Charity Cup to that Glasgow Cup triumph as Bill Struth's dominance of Scottish football showed no sign of being threatened. Gillick was seen just once more, a league match in April against Aberdeen at Ibrox as the team closed in on the title. He started this time on the right wing, helping to create a goal for the prolific Jimmy Smith in a 2-1 victory. Smith ended the season with an incredible 41 goals in just 32 league starts and, with his deputy Jimmy Fleming battering in 26 goals in all competitions (including nine in a Scottish Cup tie against Blairgowrie), it was no surprise that Gillick never got another sniff at filling his favoured centre-forward position. If he was to break into the team, it would need to be in another role and, in 1934/35, he did see his Rangers career take off.

That second season again started with Gillick in the reserves. He was given the chance to impress manager Struth in late August when Rangers took a shadow team to Parkhead to play in a benefit match for Celtic's legendary centre-forward Jimmy McGrory. Torry lined up at centre-forward with fellow youngsters Jimmy Fiddes and David Kinnear also in the forward line. On a wet Monday evening, a disappointing crowd of only 10,000 turned up to pay tribute to McGrory and the majority of spectators must have wished they had stayed at home.

The young Rangers team dominated their opponents, who also fielded an experimental line-up. It took 25 minutes for them to break the deadlock, with Gillick scoring in his first-ever top-team appearance at the home of their deadly rivals. It was a goal of simplicity and opportunism. Regular right-winger Bobby Main let fly with a firm shot that Canadian goalkeeper Joe Kennaway couldn't hold and there was the predatory Gillick on hand to tuck away the rebound.

Main added a second before half-time and the other youngsters, Fiddes and Kinnear, also got in on the scoring act. Any win over Celtic is always a source of great satisfaction for those in blue and, although this 4-0 win was only in a testimonial match, it confirmed to Struth that he had firepower aplenty in reserve for the season ahead.

Kinnear seemed to now present another obstacle to Gillick's chances of regular first-team action and the young left-winger was preferred in the first Old Firm league battle of the new season, a match which ended in a 1-1 draw. A few weeks later, the teams met again at Parkhead, this time on Monday, 24 September in the Glasgow Cup semi-final. Struth decided to play Gillick at outside-left in a match that was definitely not being treated as lightly as the McGrory testimonial. Over 31,000 attended and they witnessed a tense encounter that was finely balanced at 1-1 going into the final ten minutes. Then, Jimmy Smith won a header and the ball fell perfectly into the stride of the advancing Gillick and the 18-year-old smashed the ball into the net past goalkeeper Kellaway.

A new hero was born. Gillick not only scoring the winning goal, but he was the most dangerous forward on the field in a display that belied his tender years. One match report described his performance as 'the most pleasing feature of the game' for Rangers. This time, he wouldn't be returning to the reserves.

His lengthy run in the first team didn't include a second Glasgow Cup triumph, however, when semi-final hero Gillick was unable to prevent Partick Thistle shocking Rangers in the final thanks to a freak own goal by Jimmy Simpson. His first league goals arrived at Palmerston Park in late October in a 3-2 win over Queen of the South, a match watched by what was then a record attendance for the ground. Temporarily moved back to centre-forward, Gillick hit the home net twice in the space of a minute just before half-time with two cool finishes. A week later, he headed his first league goal at Ibrox in a win over surprise early leaders St Johnstone.

The season gradually developed into a race between the two halves of the Old Firm for the championship. It was a race in which Gillick would play a major role in the outcome. Goals from Gillick in five successive games before Christmas helped keep Rangers in front of their great rivals, the most important goal being the strike that earned a point in a surprise home draw with Hamilton Accies. After Christmas, he grabbed both goals in a thrilling 2-2 draw at Motherwell in the last fixture of 1934, his second strike being a last-gasp equaliser to rescue another point. This meant it was now just goal average separating the teams as they headed into the traditional

New Year clash of the giants. The venue was Ibrox, the attendance was a massive 83,000 and Gillick lined up on the right wing for his first experience on the pitch at Ibrox with Celtic as the visitors. It would be an eventful and memorable day.

The crowd was the biggest at the New Year fixture since the end of the Great War, reflecting the heightened level of anticipation among both sets of supporters. By half-time, it was the home fans who wore smiles. Rangers were leading thanks to a goal created by a Gillick cross and finished by Alex Venters. Celtic, meanwhile, were now handicapped by the loss of inside-forward Charlie Napier through injury and were facing playing the second 45 minutes with ten men. Celtic's goalkeeper, the Canadian Joe Kennaway, was a man inspired as he produced a string of fine saves to keep his team in the match. One Celtic fan almost didn't see the closing stages as he decided to personally congratulate the goalkeeper on his display by running on to the pitch early in the second period while the ball was out of play. He shook hands with the Celtic custodian before being grabbed by three policeman and escorted back into the away terracing, the constabulary obviously deciding it was a better punishment to see his team lose than spend the night in the cells!

The visitors continued to fight valiantly despite their numerical disadvantage, but the decisive moment arrived after 65 minutes. And it was the new hero of the blue legions, Torry Gillick, who gave them reason to celebrate. Cutting in from his wing position, he controlled the ball in an instant and drove an unstoppable shot past the despairing Kennaway before being mobbed by his ecstatic team-mates. The youngster had now scored in the biggest fixture in Scottish football at both Parkhead and Ibrox, with this goal making sure it was Rangers who would be top of the league on New Year's night.

The match had more drama to come, even though the destination of the points was no longer in doubt. Celtic were reduced to just nine men when full-back Peter McGonagle was sent off for angrily throwing the ball at the face of the prostrate Bob McPhail after the referee had penalised the Celtic man for a foul on the Rangers forward. Incredibly, the only other goal came for nine-man Celtic when, late in the game, a handball in the Rangers penalty box saw the referee point to the spot. George Paterson converted, but it was a mere consolation.

The match report in *The Scotsman* was in no doubt over the star of the match. 'The best wing on the field was the Rangers right of Gillick,' stated their reporter. But, although he was the best winger on the pitch that day, over the coming weeks manager Struth utilised the player's tremendous adaptability by fielding him occasionally at centre-forward as well as out wide. His first Scottish Cup appearance, at the end of January, saw him lead the line against Cowdenbeath at Ibrox and score twice to ensure there was no shock result as Rangers eased to a 3-1 win.

Manager Struth had used the cup tie against weaker opponents to give some fringe players their chance, with Gillick sharing a dressing room with a couple of now long-forgotten players making their competitive debuts, Sammy Roberts and Walter Hay. But with the team fighting for the title and looking to also retain the Scottish Cup, it would be back to a more familiar line-up for the majority of the rest of the season.

In the Scottish Cup, Gillick had a massive impact as the team reached another final. He was back to the right wing for the second-round win over eventual Second Division champions Third Lanark, before scoring the only goal in a nervy third-round victory over relegation-threatened St Mirren. He started this one back at the centre of the attack, the goal being a well-placed shot beyond the reach of a goalkeeper whose son would become a Rangers legend. James McCloy was given no chance by the precise Gillick finish – one that even his son, the 'Barcelona Bear' Peter, would also have struggled to get near.

This Gillick goal put Rangers into the quarter-finals, with the draw sending them on a tricky trip to Fir Park to face a Motherwell team who had come so close to defeating the champions in late December. Gillick was on the left wing this time, with the centre-forward role filled by the club's top scorer, Jimmy Smith. It was a decision few could argue with after the bustling big striker netted four goals as Rangers cruised into the semi-finals. Gillick was now two games away from a first medal in Scotland's premier cup competition.

The semi-finals saw Gillick play in front of a crowd of over 100,000 spectators for the first time. The opposition were Hearts, who had looked at one time to be genuine title contenders but were now too far behind in third place to harbour any realistic championship ambitions. They still represented a formidable challenge and the fixture attracted an attendance of 102,661 to Hampden. Gillick was close to missing the game after suffering an ankle injury ten days previously in a win over Clyde that saw him score twice in the opening 15 minutes. Passed fit on the eve of the match after missing the action the previous weekend, he took up his now regular outside-left position. Rangers would be thankful he had regained fitness, as Gillick played a vital role in proceedings.

Hearts had the advantage of the wind at their backs in the first half and they created by far the majority of chances, Rangers goalkeeper Jerry Dawson in fine form to prevent his team going behind. But the Ibrox men rallied as half-time approached and, a few minutes before the interval, the favourites struck – with their left-winger getting the goal. A Bobby Main cross went over the head of Jimmy Smith, but Gillick was rushing in at the back post, controlled the ball in an instant, held off a determined challenge by a desperate defender and rifled the ball into the net past the Wembley Wizards' goalkeeper, Jack Harkness.

Despite then having the elements in their favour in the second half, Rangers failed to take advantage and the men from Gorgie earned a replay with a surprise equaliser following a free kick. The match reports highlighted the left side of the Rangers attack – Gillick and McPhail – as the most impressive feature of the game, but it hadn't been enough to take the team through to another final. A replay was needed and the players had to wait ten days for the second match because Hampden was hosting the annual Scotland-England clash the following weekend.

Scotland won that match 2-0 with the Rangers trio of Brown, Simpson and McPhail in the team. Gillick wasn't yet seen as a realistic contender for the national team, but he was by now very much an automatic choice for Rangers and he lined up again on the left wing as another 90,000 flocked to the national stadium for the replay. He left the pitch knowing he was now set to play in his first national final after Rangers overcame their Edinburgh opponents 2-0. Gillick didn't score, although he did come close on a couple of occasions. It was McPhail, his partner on the left of the attack, who broke the deadlock before Gillick and his team-mates had to battle with just ten men for most of the second period when skipper Davie Meiklejohn was carried off injured. Forced into a more defensive role for the sake of the team, Gillick showed his great versatility as an emergency left-back. Rangers broke away to finish the contest with a goal by Bobby Main.

Waiting in the final were Hamilton Accies, who were having an excellent season in the top half of the table and who had left Ibrox with a deserved point earlier in the campaign. The final was scheduled for just ten days later, on 20 April. Meiklejohn's injury kept him out of the showpiece match, with stand-in captain Bob McPhail leading out Gillick and his team-mates. Foul weather kept many spectators away from Hampden and the crowd of just under 88,000 was the lowest for a final since 1927 but this was of little interest to Torry Gillick, who was desperate to get his hands on a first Scottish Cup medal, one of the most prized possessions in Scottish football.

He left the pitch with that precious medal in his hand and he fully deserved to claim it; both Rangers goals in a hard-fought 2-1 win were down to Gillick's crossing ability. In the first half, after captain McPhail had missed a penalty, a devilish Gillick cross caused havoc in the Hamilton defence and the prolific Jimmy Smith bundled the ball into the net. Then, with less than 20 minutes remaining and the scores level following a Hamilton equaliser, a deadly accurate Gillick corner was headed home by Smith to win the cup for Rangers.

This triumph meant the team had retained both major Scottish trophies, winning a record fourth league and cup double. A week earlier, Gillick and his team-mates had clinched the league title against Aberdeen with three games to spare. On that Saturday, Rangers had travelled to Pittodrie knowing a draw was enough to keep the championship trophy at Ibrox for another year. Gillick's 14 league goals in his 23 starts had been a big factor in the team being on the verge of glory and he lined up at outside-left in front of 17,000 spectators.

Rangers took the lead with an early Smith goal, but the scores were level by half-time. Whatever words were exchanged in the visiting dressing room had the desired effect and, within minutes of the restart, McPhail restored the Rangers lead with a blistering 18-yard shot. The title party could begin and moments later it was Gillick who added the cherry on top of the icing. His fine finish ended the match as a contest and completed a 3-1 victory. The young winger's performance was described in one match report as both 'outstanding' and 'most cunning'. He went on to score two further league goals in the remaining fixtures, both in a home draw against an Albion Rovers team who had everything to play for as they successfully avoided relegation. These took Gillick's final tally in the championship to 17 and, in all competitions, that became an even more impressive 23 when he scored his first goal in the end-of-season Charity Cup in a win over Third Lanark. He wasn't to win a first medal in that competition, though, with Partick Thistle springing an upset in their semi-final, but he had plenty more years ahead to add to his increasing medal collection. The football world was now at the feet of teenager Torry Gillick.

CHAPTER 4
A LIFETIME PARTNERSHIP

THE MOVE to Rangers wasn't the only thing that massively changed the life of Torry Gillick. Not long into his new role as a player at Scotland's biggest and most successful club, he would meet the woman who would become an even more important part of his life than the game he loved.

In 1934, the 18-year-old Gillick decided that a suitable investment for a Rangers player would be to own a motor car that befitted his status. He knew of a car showroom in the city where high-quality cars were displayed and decided to pay it a visit. The showroom was owned by a William Williamson and he employed his daughter Molly, who was also training to become a hairdresser, part-time in the showroom. When Torry had a look around, he was instantly smitten not just by the cars, but by the attractive and friendly sales assistant. Maybe it was just as well they instantly got along, as Molly found out that this would be no normal car sale – the buyer couldn't drive!

Molly was 21 years old and could drive, so she offered her services as a driving instructor, which not only helped seal the deal, but it started a lifetime partnership between them. Torry and Molly would start seeing each other as often as possible and, before long, the pair were inseparable.

The Williamsons had lived in the picturesque little Perthshire town of Creiff, which was where Mary Bothwell Williamson was born on 15 December 1913. Her mother, also Mary, preferred to call her daughter Molly and that was how she would be known for virtually her entire life. Her father's business interests meant the family needed to relocate from the tranquillity of Perthshire and they now lived in the centre of the city at 59 Park Terrace Lane, not far from Kelvingrove Park. It must have seemed a life of some luxury to many of the time, but Molly's life was impacted by several tragedies, the first of which happened in the city's Great Western Road before she and Torry had ever met. Her older brother, Jim, had a love of motorcycles. Sadly, the thrill of the open road was to prove a fatal attraction to him; he was killed in an horrific accident at the age of just 21.

Torry and Molly's courtship started at a time when his football career was really taking off. He was now a regular in a Rangers team who were challenging again for all the major honours, with the teenage footballer now having to get accustomed to fame as well as fortune. Not that footballers in the early 1930s earned anything like the vast sums now on offer, even for players with only a fraction of Gillick's talent. With many temptations for a young man earning well and in the public eye, Molly was the perfect partner to keep his feet on the ground.

He didn't particularly enjoy alcohol, but he wasn't without his vices and weaknesses. Gillick became fond of a bet, especially on the greyhounds, and his love of that sport, as well as horse racing, stayed with him for the rest of his life. He had never been what could be described as a saver, something noted by his Ibrox manager. Bill Struth always took a keen interest in the lives of his players away from the football field, and he was soon well aware of the blossoming romance in Gillick's life. When Torry admitted that he would like to put a ring on Molly's finger but didn't have the cash available to make it happen, the wily Rangers boss decided to take matters into his own hands.

Now a regular first-team star, Gillick was earning regular bonus payments on top of his weekly wage, as the team won more often than not. Struth decided that he would act as the unofficial – and top secret – savings manager for the Gillick engagement ring. He instructed the wages staff at the club to deduct a small amount from the player's wages each week and for the deducted sums to be kept in a separate account. The great traditionalist in charge of the club was very public in his view that happily married players had fewer off-field distractions and made better professionals. He also had a much less public network of spies across the city, reporting back on a regular basis on what his players got up to away from the pitch. He knew all about Gillick's regular trips to the dog track and felt that the money intended for the ring was better kept out of the teenage star's pocket until there was enough to actually buy it.

The fact that Struth was able to hide these wage deductions from the player suggests that either Torry didn't pay much attention to his wage details other than the take-home amount or possibly that he was accustomed to having money deducted for minor personal misdemeanours. Or maybe he knew all along and went along with this unusual way of saving money. However Struth managed it, by the summer of 1935 Gillick had the cash to pop the question and he and Molly were engaged.

All thoughts of a lengthy engagement were soon dispelled when Molly endured another life-changing event. In a terrible accident, her beloved mother, Mary, fell down the stairs at home and suffered a broken neck. Her injuries caused severe paralysis and confined her to bed. Her husband, William, now became her full-time carer, putting his business life very much on hold. Mr Williamson then relied heavily on their neighbours, William and Margaret Maitland, to help both at home and at work. Willie Maitland was a chauffeur in Mr Williamson's business and, as well as living next door, was a great friend. He and Margaret were a massive support during this time, along with their daughter, Ruby.

Molly would always speak of Margaret Maitland as being like a second mother and of Ruby as a sister. But even with their enormous support during this dreadful time, Torry and Molly decided that they would bring their wedding forward to Christmas Day 1935 when there would be no football fixtures, and they decided to hold the ceremony at 59 Park Lane Terrace. It became even more important when Molly's father fell seriously ill as winter set in.

Sadly, William wouldn't live to see his daughter marry. Just two weeks before her big day, he succumbed to a leaking heart valve and passed away. This happened shortly after Torry had left Glasgow for Liverpool to play for Everton, his fiancée waving him off as he travelled south by train. Molly's desolation at the loss of her father must have felt all the worse by the fact her future husband was 200 miles away and unable to be there to comfort her. His move to the English First Division had happened in a whirlwind couple of days and, as well as his football career being in upheaval, it also meant a new date was needed for the wedding, as English football had a full fixture card on 25 December. A new date of 30 December was arranged and the couple were now desperate for the date to arrive.

The wedding would be very much a bittersweet day. Willie Maitland stood in for his recently departed friend to give away the bride. His house next door was the base for Torry to get changed into his wedding suit, with a nod to his profession being included in the organisation of the day. It was agreed that the groom would rush next door for the service when summoned by a whistle. Unlike the sound of a referee whistling for his attention, this time Torry was wanting to hear it sound loud and clear.

Molly was in no doubt who she wanted to conduct the ceremony. Rev. Alexander Gillon, who was now in charge of the St Munns kirk in little Kilmun in Argyllshire, had previously been based in

Crieff where he knew the young Molly. Back then, he had agreed to officiate at her wedding whenever in the future it may be and here he was to keep his promise. Rev. Gillon pronounced them as Mr and Mrs Gillick in front of family witnesses, her uncle and aunt, John and Margaret Williamson, having travelled from the tiny village of Polton in Midlothian to the big city for the day.

With no English football over New Year, it allowed the newlyweds a few days before travelling back south for their new life together. Sadly, and typically of the year they had, there was one more blow to come. Just days after saying 'I do', Molly was saying goodbye to her mother, as Mary's broken body could fight her injuries no longer. In the space of just three weeks, Torry had seen the woman he loved suffer the cruellest of heartbreaks either side of what should have been the happiest day of her life. Not for the last time, he marvelled at her strength and he must have hoped 1936 would bring her happiness.

Once they settled into married life, times were good on Merseyside. Torry was an instant success on the pitch, helping save Everton from relegation, and Molly announced she was expecting the couple's first child as they enjoyed their new surroundings in their matrimonial home in Altway, Aintree, on the outskirts of the city of Liverpool. The couple decided that a son would be named after Molly's late father and that a girl would be given the name of Torry's beloved mother. Baby William was born towards the end of the year and he would be known to the family as Billy.

The Gillicks thoroughly enjoyed life in Aintree, home of the racecourse that stages the most famous horse race in the world. As such a keen horse racing fan, it must have been frustrating for Torry not to get to see the big race due to his football commitments. Over the coming years, however, he did manage to see plenty of Grand Nationals and, such was his popularity among the Evertonian racegoers, he often found himself as popular as any bookmaker or barman.

It was also during their time on Merseyside that the Gillicks struck up a lifelong friendship with another member of the Everton playing squad and his family. Defender Gordon Watson didn't scale the heights at Goodison Park that Torry managed as a player, but the pair enjoyed plenty of days together away from the training ground, with Molly also enjoying the friendship of Gordon's wife, Olive. In future years, even when football had taken the Gillicks back to Scotland, the Watsons remained a big part of their social life, with Gordon, Olive and their children, Hilary and Gordon Jnr, regular visitors at a time when Gordon was on the coaching staff at Goodison Park.

Gordon was mostly a reserve player during Torry's time at the club. His most regular season as half-back in the Everton first team was in the 1938/39 season when the Toffees won their first league title in seven years and what turned out to be the last championship before the outbreak of war. Torry had been a massive part of that triumph and both men must have looked forward to the 1939/40 season after such a great high, only for world events to intervene. The season did start, but national competition was abandoned after just three league games and Everton played in the regional Western League.

On 11 November 1939, Gillick scored the third goal for Everton in a Western League victory against Manchester City. The local *Evening Express* described him as 'the outstanding player on the field'. Little did he know when he left the Goodison Park pitch after the final whistle that it nearly became his last-ever football appearance. A few days later, he almost lost his life.

On Wednesday, 15 November, he was in his garage fine-tuning his car, something he enjoyed doing, while Molly was in the kitchen preparing the family dinner. Suddenly, sparks flew from the car's engine. The wooden frame of the garage caught alight and, within seconds, a significant fire took hold. Perhaps foolishly, Torry's first thought was to save the car and he tried to get into the vehicle with the idea of reversing it out of the garage before the fire destroyed it. There simply wasn't time to save the car as an inferno rapidly spread with Torry still inside the garage as the roof began to collapse.

He was now in real danger, both from the flames and from smoke inhalation, but fortunately his cries were heard and Molly rushed outside. Her actions without doubt saved him from more serious injury, perhaps even saving his life. She dragged him away from the blazing garage and rolled him on the ground to put out the flames, which were burning his clothes and skin. Torry suffered burns to his hands, arms and face, while the garage and the car were destroyed. Bootle fire brigade arrived on the scene quickly once Molly was able to leave her husband briefly to dial 999, but it was far too late to save the garage. They were able to limit the damage to the adjoining garage next door, which belonged to team-mate Walter Boyes. His garage would still need a new roof, however, although the car inside was able to be driven clear.

Torry was taken by ambulance to Walton Hospital, where his initial condition was quaintly listed as 'rather ill'. Molly also required treatment for minor burns to her hands, suffered as she bravely pulled her husband free of danger and put out the flames. She was discharged that same evening, but Torry would spend the next seven nights in hospital. Everton, who issued a statement praising the actions of Molly and the emergency services, confirmed their star winger would be missing for at least six weeks.

It would be a painful few months before Torry was seen again on a football field. Everton paid for a top skin surgeon who performed a series of skin grafts, replacing the damaged skin on his arms with tissue from his legs. There would always be some minor scarring, but the procedure was a tremendous success. In a sign of his popularity with his team-mates, before the first operation in early January, the Everton team bus stopped off in Aintree on the way to a match against Southport to allow the players to wish their colleague well. Once the initial grafts were performed, he was granted holiday leave by the club and spent five weeks back in Scotland recuperating.

Torry, Molly and young Billy stayed with his parents, giving them some quality time with their little grandson.

While back north, Gillick felt able to play the game again, so he trained with the local team, Airdrie, to get himself properly fit. With wartime rules very relaxed around the appearance of guest players, he was given permission to turn out twice for Airdrie in two cup matches against Queen's Park. He showed he had lost none of his brilliance by scoring in the first match and being a key player in the second game as his Airdrie team won through. By early March, the family were back in Aintree and he was available for Everton.

He scored on his comeback against Manchester City, but it was nearing the end of Torry Gillick's time with Everton. Just a few days after the match, it was announced that Gillick would soon return to Scotland to take up 'a post on Government service'. This entailed enlisting as a reservist with the RAF and working at an aeroplane factory to help the war effort. Due to his age and recent injuries, he would not be regarded as fit for service for at least six months, after which he would receive a medical and potentially go on the reserve list if required. He would remain a registered Everton player but would only be asked to play for them in exceptional circumstances. His return north allowed him to resume his guest career at Airdrie, where he played occasionally until the end of the season.

He did answer an SOS from Everton in late May when they had a player crisis for a cup match at Fulham, spending 18 hours in trains to get down to London to make a goalscoring Everton appearance in a 5-2 defeat. But the family were now back where they were most at home, living in Gartness, with Torry making the occasional appearance again for Airdrie.

But for the 1940/41 football season, things on and off the field would change greatly for the Gillicks. In the summer of 1940, Everton agreed to allow their player to join Rangers as a guest, reuniting Gillick with Bill Struth almost five years after the Ibrox boss allowed him to leave the club. Under new rules issued by the Football League in England, this now had to be done in the form of a transfer, meaning Everton could not summon their player back at all during the season. Everton insisted the player's insurance was covered by Rangers, but they agreed there would be no transfer fee, with the arrangement being for one season and Gillick living north of the border and working for the government.

Meanwhile, during the new season Molly found herself expecting the couple's second child. As Torry was quick to point out, this one wouldn't be born in England! In 1941, Molly gave birth to a daughter, the couple keeping their previous promise by naming her Isabella after the baby's grandmother. Isabella was born in the family home, which housed three generations of the Gillick family. Perhaps to avoid any confusion, the baby would be known as Isobel by the family. Despite the hardship and the suffering of war, the Gillicks were as content as they had ever been. Torry was back playing for the club he had never wanted to leave and life at home was full of the joy of having young children.

Success on the field came along quickly and often, Rangers dominating the wartime Scottish football scene. And as Torry gathered more medals and scored more memorable goals, a second daughter followed less than a year after Isobel's arrival, with Molly born in 1942. Also that year, Rangers secured Gillick's services for as long as the war lasted. In 1945, as the world finally emerged from the horrors of war, the Gillicks also had a further reason to celebrate as a second son – Larry, named after Torry's father – arrived. It took until 1946 for national football competition to resume and, by then, Gillick had completed a permanent transfer back to Rangers, making him the first – and only – player ever to have been brought to the club twice by William Struth. The iconic Rangers manager, now in his 70s, was still the man who ruled inside Ibrox but, despite his iron reputation, he said simply of Gillick 'he makes me laugh'. With a permanent move back to Ibrox confirmed, the Gillicks were able to search for a home in the city rather than living in Gartness with Torry's parents. They bought a lovely little cottage in the small suburb of Swinton and moved the family there in early 1947. They also bought an area of land in nearby Baillieston, as Torry looked beyond his playing career. This would be where he would later set up the business he ran after his football days were behind him.

The cottage became an unofficial meeting place for the Rangers players in the following months, the team holding regular sessions together to talk tactics and strategy for upcoming matches. This may seem strange to modern football fans, who are accustomed to seeing managers in tracksuits barking out tactical instructions, with their backroom staff holding clipboards with formations on them. In the late 1940s, as had been the case for much of the Struth era at the club, the senior players were left to decide tactics, with the manager trusting them to alter their approach as they saw fit. Struth was certainly in charge of club discipline, fitness, transfers and team selection, but men like Jock Shaw, George Young, Willie Waddell and Torry Gillick were the brains behind how the team would play.

Life seemed idyllic for the family, with Torry starring for a Rangers side that was collecting trophy after trophy, a wonderful home life in Swinton with so many friends around the family and the four children the centre of it all. Then in April 1947, the first blow of a double tragedy struck. Rangers had reached the final of the first Scottish League Cup, with the final against Aberdeen to be played on Saturday, 5 April. Just 24 hours before the big match, for which more than 120,000 tickets had been sold, Torry received the devastating news that his father, Lawrence, had passed away at the age of 55.

Being the only son, Torry had the responsibility to both comfort his mother and make arrangements for the funeral. At Ibrox, his manager left the decision on whether he was available to play up to the player. After much soul-searching and a long and emotional chat with Molly, he decided not to withdraw his name from the team and to take to the Hampden pitch. Most of the Hampden crowd would have been totally unaware of the turmoil in the mind of the

Rangers number eight and the majority of the spectators went home happy after watching Rangers win 4-0, with Torry showing his great strength of character by scoring the opening goal.

The funeral was held a few days later at Old Monklands cemetery, a place where the family would sadly return only months later. Young Isobel was a typical little girl, full of mischief and fun. But in the summer of 1947, she started to tire easily and bruises were appearing on her arms and legs after the slightest of bumps. The diagnosis of leukaemia devastated everyone and, despite the best efforts of doctors, this was an illness in post-war Britain that was effectively a death sentence. Torry and Molly spent every hour they could with their precious elder daughter as her little body gradually lost the fight against a cruel and heartless disease.

Isobel's brave battle ended on Friday, 30 January 1948 when she was just six years old. Her tragic passing left its mark on the family from that day onwards, Torry especially being broken-hearted and angry at how fate had taken away his beautiful little girl. For many years afterwards, he became almost paranoid about any bruise the other children suffered and he ordered that all photographs which featured Isobel be taken off display at the family home as he simply could not bear the pain of seeing them.

Isobel died on a Friday and Rangers had a match the following afternoon. As it happened, the fixture on 31 January was no ordinary game. Rangers were locked in a titanic battle for the league championship with an excellent Hibs team and were due to travel to Easter Road for a highly anticipated game that was regarded as crucial in determining the destination of the title. Defending champions Rangers knew defeat might be a blow from which they would not recover, but manager Struth again left the decision to Gillick to whether he felt able to take part.

He really should have refused to take to the Easter Road pitch; his mind and body were simply elsewhere. But Molly was left to grieve without her husband that Saturday afternoon, as Torry took to the field at Easter Road, his grief still at its rawest. In the following week's Ibrox match programme against Leith Athletic, the club printed a heartfelt tribute to the player and expressed their sympathy for his tragic loss. It quoted Gillick as telling his manager: 'I'll play at Easter Road. I don't want to let the boys down.' The attendance figure was just short of 53,000 and was a record for the Edinburgh ground at the time. But Torry was a man all alone. It was absolutely no surprise when he looked miles off the pace of the game. He lost tackles he should have won, he didn't make the clever runs associated with his game and his passing was badly off target. The *Glasgow Herald* report of the game stated that he 'showed all the signs of a tired and troubled man' and that he was 'not his usual crafty quicksilver self'. He rushed home as soon as he could after the final whistle sounded, Hibs having scored the only goal of the game with almost the last kick of the match. The Edinburgh team would go on to take the crown by just two points. Then, on the Monday, Torry and Molly were inconsolable as the little coffin was lowered into the same lair at Old Monklands as Isobel's grandfather had been buried in less than a year before. Life, of course, had to go on. And life would still hold some wonderful memories and enjoyable times. But the Gillicks would always have that small part of their hearts broken from then on.

The cottage in Swinton was now a place they associated with the loss of their precious daughter and, when given the opportunity to move again, Torry and Molly gratefully accepted the offer. The Rangers board of directors had a great friend in John Lawrence, who owned a thriving housebuilding business. Lawrence would be voted on to the board in years to come and eventually became club chairman in the early 1960s. The club were given a discount on several properties in the sought-after neighbourhood of Bearsden for staff and players and Torry was one of a number of Ibrox stars who moved there.

It must have been a dream location for any Rangers fan who collected autographs. In close proximity to the Gillick home in Bearsden's Hillfoot area were the families of George Young, Ian McColl and Torry's partner on the Rangers right wing, Willie Waddell. At Christmas, Willie Thornton's house next door would be used to hide the gifts for the Gillick children. Across the street lived a great player from just before Torry's first spell at the club, former captain Tommy Muirhead, who now wrote for the *Daily Express*.

As the new decade dawned, Torry had also struck up a personal and professional friendship with a Bathgate-based road haulage businessman William Alston and this was to lead to Torry discovering another great love of his life. Alston was a particularly popular visitor to the Gillick house, as his network of contacts meant he was able to get hold of treats like crisps and sweets that were still rationed in post-war Britain. Just a few months after the tragic death of Isobel, Alston telephoned Torry to tell him he had found a beautiful holiday location in the north-west of Scotland. The picturesque little village of Dornie had become the Alston family's favourite destination for breaks and, with its stunning scenery and plentiful fishing waters, they recommended it as the perfect getaway from the pressures of top-class football and the overwhelming grief the Gillicks were still enduring.

Alston suggested Torry book the Loch Duich Hotel and it took one look for the Gillicks to fall in love with the place. Dornie became the family's regular hideaway, the place they would go whenever they needed a break and wanted to get away from it all. With the love of fishing Torry had inherited from his father and his Uncle Bob, it was the perfect place and the surrounding rivers and lochs would be his favourite relaxation spots for the rest of his days.

It wasn't just the location that stole their hearts; they also made great friends there and forged bonds that lasted a lifetime. Although they used the recommended hotel for their first trips north, the family had become great friends with a local family who owned a bed and breakfast. Rockfield was run by Katie Macaskill, whose family would become a massive part of Torry and Molly's lives.

The five Macaskill brothers – Donald, Alistair, John, Norman and Roddy – and their sisters, Katie and Chrissie, spent countless hours with the Gillicks, the brothers enjoying days and nights on the shores of the local lochs with Torry as they tried to outwit the local salmon. Favourite spots included Loch Duich and Loch Long, as well as Torry's favourite solo spots on the banks of the River Croe at Morvich, and the Rivers Ling and Elchaig at Killilan. The whole family looked forward to their trips north to Rockfield.

A particular favourite stretch of river for salmon was in the nearby Inverinate and Killilan estates. The Killilan estate was owned by the Douglas family. Mrs Douglas was related to the Wills Tobacco company owners, the locals christening her family boat the SS *Woodbine*. Torry rented an area of the river from them for many years and, after spending hours there in all weathers, he would proclaim himself 'happy as a lark, and wouldn't call the king my brother' regardless of whether his patience had been rewarded with any fish.

The early post-war years had contained too much heartbreak, but they also were the years in which the Gillicks started to build a life of happiness and memories after Torry's football career was over.

CHAPTER 5

FROM CLYDESIDE TO MERSEYSIDE

WHEN RANGERS kicked off the 1935/36 season with a typically dominant 6-0 Ibrox win over newly promoted Arbroath on 10 August 1935, they were the masters of all they surveyed in Scottish football and Torry Gillick, still only 19, was a fixture in the team. He started the match back on the right wing in the absence of Bobby Main, which allowed a rare start for another youngster, David Kinnear, wide on the left. Jimmy Smith smashed home yet another hat-trick on the day, with Gillick scoring the second goal with a well-placed shot shortly before half-time.

Gillick's versatility was very much in evidence in the opening weeks of the new season. Before August was complete, he also filled the inside-right and outside-left positions as manager Struth juggled his forward options due to multiple absences. By mid-October, Gillick had played in all of the first dozen games in the league, completing the set of all five forward roles when playing inside-left in a disappointing home defeat to Celtic. It was a day that saw an unfamiliar Rangers line-up due to injuries, with reserve players Alex Winning and Sammy Roberts drafted in to fill the gaps left by several missing regulars.

Gillick showed he still had his old Petershill goalscoring magic at centre-forward when notching a fine double in a handsome win against Dunfermline in the absence of Jimmy Smith. The extent of the injuries at the club meant he played alongside some now long-forgotten team-mates as several reserve players were given opportunities. One of these was the Egyptian inside-forward Mohammed Latif, who made his first and only competitive Rangers appearance in a 1-1 draw at Easter Road on 14 September.

Two weeks later, Gillick scored the decisive second goal as Rangers reached yet another Glasgow Cup Final by defeating Clyde 2-0. This set up an Old Firm showdown on 12 October 1935, giving Rangers and Gillick the chance to avenge the recent league defeat. He didn't realise it at the time, but this would be Gillick's last Old Firm start and last cup final appearance as a Rangers player until the early 1940s. Typically, he would leave his mark.

The 50,000 crowd inside Ibrox had seen 20-year-old Jimmy Fiddes open the scoring in the second half, when just a few minutes later Gillick made sure the cup would return to the Ibrox trophy room with a goal of sheer impudence. As Celtic goalkeeper John Kennaway was organising his defence at a Rangers corner kick, Gillick whipped in a vicious inswinging effort that sailed over the helpless Kennaway and into the far top corner of the net. A devastating display of cheek and ability, one that saw Gillick mobbed by his smiling team-mates who knew more silverware had been won. There was no doubt that the stiff wind helped Gillick and he attempted the feat twice more and very nearly succeeded. The match report in the *Glasgow Herald* stated Gillick had been 'outstanding'. This was something of an understatement.

Bob McPhail had missed the match, becoming the latest of the Ibrox big-hitters to fall foul of the injury curse. Gillick was doing all he could to help maintain a title challenge, but inconsistency in team selection and the absence of so many important players were severely impacting results. Gillick's second-half goal at Ibrox helped overcome a spirited Hamilton team in mid-November. It was a goal that turned out to be his last at Ibrox in a Rangers shirt for nearly five years.

On 7 December, Rangers travelled to Perth to take on St Johnstone, who were managed by the legendary ex-Rangers captain Tommy Muirhead. The top of the league table was extremely tight, Rangers sitting in third place behind Aberdeen and Celtic and knowing they couldn't afford to slip up at a tricky venue. Gillick was back in his most common position at outside-left and, on a frosty, rock-hard pitch, he scored the winning goal just before half-time when his precise finish from a clever Alex Venters pass made the score 2-1. Rangers held out in the second half, down to ten men for the last half-hour after an injury to defender Jimmy Simpson. Rangers had now played 19 games in the league, Gillick starting all

17 he had been available for. He would have left the pitch at Muirton Park delighted to grab the all-important goal and looking forward to the upcoming festive fixtures. However, in the background, moves to take him away from Ibrox were nearing completion. Muirton Park would be the ground where the first Rangers career of Torry Gillick came to an end.

Both Everton and Aston Villa had representatives watching Gillick at Perth, with both clubs eager to lure him south. There were also rumours of interest from Manchester City.

Everton and Villa were both in the bottom three of the First Division and were desperate to bolster their attacking firepower to avoid the disaster of relegation.

Everton had recently made an offer to Rangers, one which manager Struth took little time in rejecting. He insisted a fee of £8,000 would be required if the Merseyside club were serious and, after Everton had suffered a calamitous 6-1 defeat to West Brom at the same time as Gillick was scoring the winning goal at Muirton Park, acting club secretary Theo Kelly indicated Everton were willing to meet the asking price. It was a record fee for the Goodison Park club and Kelly arranged to travel to Glasgow on the Monday to conclude the transfer.

Gillick was totally unaware of this activity and reported for training on Monday, 9 December as usual. When summoned to the manager's office, he must have been wondering what he had done wrong; perhaps he had been too slow in putting on his bowler hat!

Struth never fully explained his reasoning for allowing his young star player to leave Rangers. It might be that it was simply too good an offer to turn down, with the club having plenty of other forwards on the books. It might be that the iron fist of Ibrox had decided Gillick did not meet his demanding standards off the pitch. Perhaps it was Struth thinking a move away and a handsome signing-on fee would be best for the young man's future following his engagement.

It certainly couldn't have been down to unhappiness at Gillick's performances on the park. Whatever the reason, Gillick was faced with a momentous decision to make and was given little time to decide. With Rangers not standing in his way if he wanted to leave, he opted to accept Everton's offer and move south.

After 28 goals in 55 league and Scottish Cup appearances and with a league title, a Scottish Cup winner's badge and two Glasgow Cup successes to his name, Torry Gillick was no longer a Rangers player.

A whirlwind day wasn't yet complete. With the transfer agreed, but not yet made public, Gillick and fiancée Molly travelled by car to visit his parents in Airdrie to inform them of the move south before they read it in the newspapers. Glasgow was in the grip of winter, with the roads in the area somewhat treacherous to navigate. They safely made the journey to Lanarkshire but, on their return into the city, the car skidded on ice in the Baillieston area and struck a lamppost. It's probably fair to say that the weather had been by far the major factor in the accident, although Gillick was driving in difficult conditions at the end of a day when he was likely still in something of a state of shock at how it had unfolded.

The car windscreen shattered on the driver's side and, while Molly escaped without injury, Torry suffered cuts to his hands, having raised them in front of his face on impact. The player was quick to play down the incident, contacting his new employers the next morning to inform them of the accident but stressing that his injuries were 'very, very slight' and that there was no risk to him being able to play the following weekend when Everton were due to face Leeds United at Goodison Park.

It would not, of course, be Torry's last incident involving a car.

He left Glasgow for Liverpool by train, waved off by Molly, who was accompanied by manager Struth, which strongly suggested that the Rangers boss had no personal issues with the player and that the sale was down to financial considerations.

Gillick was soon being welcomed to Goodison Park by the legendary centre-forward 'Dixie' Dean in a photoshoot for the press and it was announced that the new signing would start on the right wing against Leeds with fellow Scot Billy Miller, previously of Partick Thistle, his partner on the right side of the attack. This decision was made at the regular meeting of the club selectors, Everton not having a manager at this time in their history. His signing was the main story in the sports pages of the local press, with great interest in the Scottish teenage prodigy who had been signed for a record fee.

The Merseyside press informed the Liverpool public that Everton's new forward was 5ft 7in tall, weighed 10st 10lb and had made his Rangers debut alongside current Everton favourite Alex Stevenson. The *Liverpool Echo* described him as one of the brightest stars of the younger school of Rangers players and, indeed, the most versatile forward in Scotland. Fans were told that his best position was centre-forward but that his game time there had been limited due to the imposing figure of Jimmy Smith and that he tended to be played on the left wing where there had been no regular starter for the position.

The fee has widely been reported over the years as £8,000; however, the official minutes of the Everton board meeting of 10 December 1935 at the Exchange Hotel in Liverpool stated the fee was £6,500 with a weekly wage of £8 plus a £10 signing-on fee. The signing-on fee seems particularly low even for the times – it was half the fee paid to the player when he left Petershill for Ibrox – but the weekly wage he would now receive was a significant increase. There is some doubt over the accuracy of the club's minuted account of the transfer and whether both the transfer fee and the signing-on fee were documented as lower than the actual numbers for accounting purposes or to persuade supporters the club had negotiated a good deal.

Regardless of the exact cost to the club, Everton were in a precarious position in the table. The fans were looking for a saviour. The pressure was on 19-year-old Gillick to be that man.

Just under 29,000 were inside Goodison on Saturday, 14 December to see Gillick's bow in the blue of Everton. They saw a solid but mainly quiet debut, with Leeds the better team for long spells and Gillick seeing little of the ball in dangerous areas. He did force a fine save from visiting goalkeeper Albert McInroy with a low shot in the second half as well as providing a fine cross for a near miss by Nat Cunliffe. Neither side could find a goal on a bumpy and frosty pitch but the 0-0 draw at least arrested Everton's losing run and most onlookers agreed that their new young winger had shown enough promise for there to be optimism that the record fee had been well spent. This initial impression was shared by reporters in the Liverpool press, with the piece in the *Liverpool Echo* describing him as a 'thinking footballer' who 'the longer he played, the better he became'.

Gillick's first away match, the following Saturday, proved to be highly eventful. The opposition were Birmingham City at St Andrew's, with Gillick's versatility already being utilised by the Everton selectors, who switched him to the left wing. As was customary, the team were to travel by train, with the club party all booked on the 9.40am from Liverpool Lime Street station. This should have given plenty of time for the players to have lunch in Birmingham ahead of the match. Unfortunately, the train was badly delayed by fog, with club secretary Kelly forced to order 'luncheon baskets' for each of the party as the train sat at Crewe awaiting permission to proceed any further. By the time it arrived at Wolverhampton, the train was over 90 minutes delayed, so the players were instructed to get changed into their playing kit. Their eventual arrival in Birmingham at 2.10pm was just 20 minutes before kick-off and onlookers stared in amazement as a group of footballers wearing their playing strip and carrying their civilian clothes raced along the platform to be greeted by waiting cars, which drove off at full speed.

The match was eventually delayed until 2.40pm and, with floodlighting at British football grounds still two decades away, the clubs agreed that, to make up for the lost ten minutes, there would be no half-time interval. Perhaps unsurprisingly, after the chaos of the journey, Everton found themselves 3-1 down at the changeover, with the match ending in a 4-2 loss. The second half, however, did see another milestone in the Gillick career when he scored his first goal in English football. There were just five minutes remaining and the points were already long gone, but Gillick gave the travelling Everton fans something to cheer by cutting inside and crashing home a fine shot. It was a bright end to a crazy and disappointing day.

His team might have been well beaten, but several match reports were full of praise for Gillick's display. The *Evening Express,* in particular, singled out Gillick as 'an enthusiastic youth with a wise and cool head on his shoulders'. Their report also mentioned his mastery of the ball despite the icy conditions and how he 'let the ball do the work' in his range of passing. Only two games into his

Everton career and it was already obvious that Gillick was in the team to stay.

Everton's next fixture was at Sheffield Wednesday on Christmas Day, the original date for Torry and Molly's wedding in Glasgow. The ceremony had been postponed to 30 December after Gillick's transfer from Rangers but, ironically, the Hillsborough pitch was declared unplayable after two inches of snow had fallen the previous night. However, the Boxing Day return fixture against Wednesday at Goodison Park did go ahead and Gillick enjoyed both a first win and a first goal in front of his home crowd when he headed Everton's third goal in a thrilling 4-3 victory. The win was all the more remarkable considering goalkeeper Ted Sagar received a nasty knee injury in a collision that forced him to play the first 12 minutes of the second half at outside-left while he tried to shake off the effects. Winger Albert Geldard briefly took over in goal, conceding the third Wednesday goal. The last match Gillick would play as a single man would be against Derby County two days later at the Baseball Ground. County had obviously identified the young Scot as the biggest danger to their defence and he was on the receiving end of some tackles that verged on brutality. After only being passed fit to play on the morning of the match after taking a knock against Wednesday, he limped forlornly to the dressing room at half-time. Some of his team-mates tried to convince him to stay there for the remainder of the match, so concerned were they by his condition. Gillick, however, was having none of it and he completed the match and helped his team to a valuable point in a 3-3 draw. It was a bruised and battered Gillick who would take his marriage vows 48 hours later.

With no 'Ne'erday' football in England, the newlyweds were able to enjoy a few days together before the first match of 1936. Their joy was shortlived, however, with the passing of Molly's mother on 2 January back in Glasgow. For Mary Williamson, the pain was over, but for Molly – whose father had passed away only weeks earlier – it meant more devastating heartache at what should have been the happiest time of her life.

After this second tragedy for Molly in a matter of weeks, Gillick did much soul searching before deciding he would play for Everton on the Saturday. After enjoying the blood and thunder of the Old Firm derby in Glasgow, Gillick would now get his first taste of the Merseyside equivalent when Liverpool were the first-footers at Goodison. A big crowd of more than 52,000 saw honours finish even, the 0-0 draw leaving Everton second from bottom and still with very real relegation worries. Showing incredible character at a time of family mourning, Gillick came the closest of anyone on the field to grabbing a winner when his first-half shot struck the post.

When his first appearance in the FA Cup went badly wrong the following week, with a dismal defeat to Preston, it looked like Gillick only had a relegation battle to look forward to until May. But a fine unbeaten run of ten matches from the start of February helped ease the club's fears. Gillick more than played his part in this crucial period, with goals against Middlesbrough, Arsenal, Grimsby and a double against Manchester City in a cracking 2-2 draw at Goodison. His partner now on the left side of the attack was a former Rangers team-mate, Alex Stevenson, a diminutive and clever inside-forward who hailed originally from Dublin. They had only ever played together once in a competitive match for the Ibrox club, Torry's league debut 4-3 win at Firhill in September 1933. Now they were playing a key role in preserving Everton's top-flight status.

By the final day of the season and a home match against their cup conquerors Preston, Everton still needed a draw to be mathematically safe, although several results would have needed to go against them and any defeat would have had to have been by a heavy margin. Gillick was in fine form as they crushed the men from Deepdale 5-0, with Everton ending 1935/36 in 16th place, four points clear of the drop. The teenage Gillick could look back on his first campaign south of the border with satisfaction, scoring nine times in 23 starts and already being regarded as a key man in Everton's rebuilding programme as they looked to challenge at the other end of the table in the future.

The close season would begin with a tour to Germany, a country now ruled by the iron fist of Adolf Hitler, and it would be memorable for Gillick in many ways, on and off the pitch. It all started with the touring party booked aboard the liner *New York,* which set sail from Southampton on 8 May bound for Hamburg. The ship was luxurious and paid for by the German FA, with the players enjoying time in the onboard gymnasium and swimming pools during the voyage.

At 9.50pm on that first day, the vessel collided with the Dutch steamer *Alpard* off the coast of Belgium. Within 20 minutes, the stricken steamer had disappeared into the depths of the North Sea. All 26 on board were rescued, with eight crew managing to climb aboard the *New York* via rope ladders and the remaining 18 lucky survivors being picked up by the *New York* lifeboat and taken aboard the liner. Ernest Green, the club director in charge of the Everton travelling party, spoke of his admiration for the calm way the *New York* crew had dealt with a potentially catastrophic situation and of how his players were unaffected and looking forward to their opening game. Player Charlie Leyfield, who occupied the opposite wing to Gillick on matchday, told reporters how the players had been in the ballroom when they felt the collision and had all rushed on deck to watch the rescue. He also spoke of how passengers cheered the lifeboat as it returned safely aboard and of a collection taken among the passengers to assist those involved.

The first match of the tour was due to be played on the evening after this incident, the first of five matches against combined German teams comprising players shortlisted for the upcoming Olympic Games being held in the country. The matches were played in Hamburg, Duisburg, Frankfurt, Stuttgart and Nuremburg and honours ended up even after two wins apiece and the final match finishing in a hard-fought 1-1 draw. The Everton team travelled between cities by train and on one leg of their tour they found their train diverted into a siding for around an hour, with no official explanation. It turned out that the line was being cleared to allow a train carrying Hitler and his entourage to pass without the need for it to stop. It would be the closest Gillick would come to seeing the German leader, whose reign of terror would be responsible for ending his Everton career a few years later. It was a chilling reminder of the times that the match in Stuttgart took place in the sinisterly named Adolf Hitler Stadium.

Gillick played in all five matches of the tour, his highlight being a man-of-the-match performance in the third game of the series in Frankfurt on 16 May. Everton won 3-1, with Gillick's two goals the difference between the teams. This was his last-ever match as a teenager, as three days later Gillick turned 20. The occasion was marked during a dinner held that evening, when officials of both the club and the German hosts were present to hear Everton defender Charlie Gee raise a toast in Gillick's name, with the shy Scot giving a much shorter reply before sitting back down. A report of the dinner in the Liverpool press described him as 'overcome by the spontaneous greeting he received'. This showed the popularity Gillick already enjoyed among his Goodison team-mates, a popularity shared on the terraces after his impressive debut season. He had not only made 23 league appearances and notched nine goals, helping the club preserve their top-flight status. He had also entertained those watching and given hope for the future. His career on Merseyside was off to an excellent start.

Torry had already earned a new temporary nickname among the players a few days earlier in the tour; he was dubbed 'Foreign secretary' Gillick after he was spotted carrying a weighty book, which one dressing room joker compared to the Locarno Pact – a series of treaties signed by the main European countries a few years earlier which were designed to ensure peace on the continent. Sadly, that peace would turn out to be as temporary as the Gillick nickname.

The following season of 1936/37 would see Gillick almost an ever-present, missing only one league game in the entire campaign, appearing 41 times and scoring 14 goals. It wasn't enough to particularly improve the team's fortunes, however, as Everton finished a lowly 17th in the First Division. Players had returned to training on 30 July optimistic for the season ahead after their strong finish to the last campaign, although the supporters were not convinced and were anxious for new blood to be recruited. Many felt that Torry, along with several team-mates, were still too young to make any real impression.

There was pre-season speculation over which position the versatile Gillick would be deployed in and whether he would fill the troublesome outside-right berth, a spot he had so far only appeared in on his debut against Leeds. In the customary Blues versus Whites trial matches, he lined up on the left and then right and scored in both games. Everton then headed to Highbury to open the season in a positive frame of mind.

It was not to be, however, with Arsenal prevailing 3-2 on the day. The match was notable for the legendary 'Dixie' Dean equalling the all-time scoring record for the club, while several match reports noted that Gillick was again in great form. This loss kicked off a thoroughly unsatisfactory season for the club, with only a few bright days. In early season, however, Gillick must have thought things were going well both for the club and himself. In the space of a fortnight, he scored four times, a double strike in a crazy 6-4 defeat at Sheffield Wednesday being sandwiched between a goal in a comfortable 3-0 victory over Brentford and a late winner at Bolton.

There were some highlights to come, such as a 7-0 win against Derby on Christmas Day 1936 and a thumping 7-1 win against Leeds in March in which Torry notched one of the goals. But, as was typical during a wildly inconsistent season, a few days after hitting Derby for seven, Everton were well and truly beaten 3-1 at the Baseball Ground in the reverse fixture. Despite this dismal loss, it was a match notable for a Gillick display described as 'superlative' by one reporter who lamented that, if only the rest of the forwards had been on his wavelength, the scoreline may have been different.

A local derby win over Liverpool in September was another match which saw Gillick receive high praise in several reports. The victory had highlighted Torry's versatility and game intelligence, Liverpool spending the afternoon chasing shadows as he repeatedly switched from the wing to centre-forward during the match. This unpredictable habit of leaving his wing and looking to cause havoc further infield wasn't always appreciated by traditionalists who wanted their wide men to remain out on the touchlines and it occasionally took his team-mates by surprise, too. On the day, he missed two great chances to score after drifting into the Liverpool box and, if he had converted either of them, the terrace tacticians would no doubt have then approved.

Nineteen defeats in the 42 league matches meant Everton remained far nearer the bottom than the top despite scoring more goals than Charlton and Arsenal, who finished second and third, respectively. Gillick and the forwards were obviously not where the problem lay. After a run of ten matches without a win to end the league campaign, it was obvious that changes were needed if Everton were to become challengers for silverware. The *Liverpool Echo* sports columnist known as 'Bee' summed up a dismal season, lambasting the team's defensive frailties and habit of missing easy chances. But he was crystal clear there was one player who should remain an automatic choice and be played more often in the role he was best suited to. 'Gillick's place is at outside-right,' he wrote, adding that, if he was selected there regularly, 'the inside men should get plenty of goals.' As well as the lowly league finish, there would be no joy in the FA Cup. Gillick and Everton were knocked out by Tottenham in a fifth-round replay at White Hart Lane. But despite the club's poor fortunes, Gillick's displays had attracted the attention of the national team selectors and, at the season's conclusion, Torry turned out for Scotland against both Austria and Czechoslovakia. He then joined up with his club-mates for a tour of Denmark.

Everton remained undefeated over the three matches, with two wins and a draw against a Danish Select team, but they again had drama to contend with on the return boat trip. A stabbing incident took place between two passengers, with the perpetrator jumping overboard. It was some time before he was rescued and detained in a cargo net until a police launch arrived. Not surprisingly, the journey home was delayed by six hours.

The 1937/38 season was one of frustration for Gillick. His start to the campaign was seriously disrupted by injury and he did not make his first league appearance until the 11th match, against Leeds at Goodison on 16 October. In the end, he only appeared 14 times in the league, scoring three goals, and although the Toffees improved their final league standing to 14th, they were still falling well short of expectations.

Torry's woes started after he sustained an injury in the second practice match of pre-season, the traditional Blues v Whites encounter. He limped off and initially it was thought he had injured a tendon, but it was then found to be something more serious. He was admitted to hospital and, after the knee was X-rayed, a specialist diagnosed a misplaced cartilage. In the 1930s, this was considered a serious injury; unlike today, when he would probably only have missed a couple of weeks. In 1937, it involved an operation with a lengthy recuperation period. In Gillick's case, it meant he missed two months before his October return.

After Gillick played and scored the following week in a 2-1 win at Grimsby, the directors took the decision to remove him from the first team to help him regain his confidence. This highlighted the issues of teams being chosen by a committee, with the local press claiming that removing him from team so quickly might have exactly the opposite impact to what was intended. There was some speculation in the press that Everton were looking for a player to occupy their troublesome outside-left berth but that, if Gillick returned to form, this would no longer be a requirement.

Following a spell playing in the reserves in the Central League, Torry returned to the first team at the beginning of December against Charlton at the Valley. It was not to be a happy return, as Everton went down 3-1. It was noted in one press report that Gillick showed 'nice positional sense but accomplished very little'. This was surely unsurprising given his sporadic appearances over the previous four months. He dropped out of the team again in mid-December and, back in the reserves, his struggle for form continued. This was the pattern for the remainder of season, with Gillick in and out of the first team. It was the first time in his career that Gillick found himself no longer a regular, something that frustrated him greatly.

To his credit, he refused to allow his standards to drop while playing in the second string, scoring several important goals in the reserve matches he took part in. Among these were a double on Christmas Day at Chesterfield in a 2-0 win watched by a handful of spectators. A far cry from the massive attendances Torry had been used to entertaining.

The season was a huge struggle for Everton and they only secured their continued First Division status in the penultimate match of the season when an Alex Stevenson hat-trick inspired a 5-2 victory over Portsmouth at Goodison. The opinion column in one of the local newspapers commented: 'It has been a poor season from a playing point of view and Everton's position in the table is causing much worry both inside and outside the boardroom.' One of those worries must surely have been in the mind of Torry Gillick, wondering when he would return to the first team on a regular basis and get back to doing what he enjoyed most.

The end of season, though, would bring a real treat for Torry with a return to his old stomping ground of Ibrox for the Empire Exhibition Cup, a tournament organised to coincide with the Empire Exhibition being held at Bellahouston Park. Everton were one of four English sides invited along with Brentford, Chelsea and Sunderland. They would face Scottish rivals in the shape of Rangers, Celtic, Hearts and Aberdeen.

Everton were drawn against Rangers and eased to a comfortable 2-0 win, with the Ibrox cause not helped by an injury to goalkeeper Jerry Dawson, who had to be replaced in goal by captain Jimmy Simpson for the final half an hour of the match. Despite this, the newspapers praised Everton in earning 'a wholly conclusive victory' against a Rangers side who were 'poorly served in attack'.

In the semi-final against Aberdeen, Torry scored after only five seconds as the Toffees went on to win 3-2 in what was a much sterner test than the win over Rangers. It was a bittersweet match for Gillick, however, as he sustained an injury which forced him to miss the final. The frustration at sitting on the sidelines would have been compounded, given the opposition and the final score. Celtic won 1-0 after extra time.

Everton thanked Queen's Park, Rangers and Skelmorlie Football Club for their support in preparing for the final and also left a lasting impression during their stay at the Skelmorlie Hydro Hotel where staff and residents were completely charmed by the good behaviour of the players who mixed with guests, including joining in a whist drive.

Preparations for the upcoming 1938/39 campaign were reported as being happy, carefree and lacking in elaboration, as the players went through their paces for the new season. This would be a fresh start for Torry, too, after the trials of the previous season and his priority was simply to nail down a regular place again. His chances of a starting berth looked bright, with Irish right-winger Albert Geldard allowed to leave the club to sign for Bolton Wanderers. This strongly suggested that the right-wing position was seen as belonging to Gillick for the upcoming campaign, a role the player himself preferred to wide on the left.

It wasn't the wing positions that most worried loyal Evertonians, however. Concerns among the Everton faithful focussed on a defence which had conceded 75 goals the previous season and, to make progress up the table, that would need to be addressed as a priority. It would be a season in which Gillick and the supporters saw all their wishes come true.

It got off to a promising start, Everton beating Liverpool 2-1 in the Jubilee Fund match with goals from Stevenson and Tommy Lawton before 17,468 spectators. The game was staged to celebrate the 60th anniversary of the club being formed by a group of youths linked to St Domingo Methodist Chapel. The league season opened at Bloomfield Road with a comfortable 2-0 win over Blackpool, both goals coming in the opening 20 minutes and Gillick playing a starring role. After the match, new captain Jock Thomson was quoted as saying, 'There is a wonderful spirit in the team and immense confidence has been gained by the club's great performances in the Glasgow Exhibition games.' Everton gained some real momentum, rattling off six wins on the bounce, which included away victories at Highbury and Villa Park. The latter of these saw the Toffees play magnificent football which was reported as the best seen from an Everton team for many a year. The concerns over the defence were also abating, with only three goals conceded in those opening games.

Despite this fantastic start, Gillick was attracting occasional criticism from the hard-to-please punters on the terraces, as he had not maintained his form of the opening match. There was a view he performed better away from home and fans were frustrated by his habit of moving inside and vacating his position on the wing. However, the considered thinking of many within the game was that this switch of position was both innovative and effective and that it was up to the inside-forward to cover Torry's slot on the wing when he took advantage of space infield to create danger.

When Portsmouth were thrashed 5-1 at Goodison, Everton had set a new league record, becoming the first team to win the opening six matches in a First Division campaign. Even the most fickle fan was impressed now, with glowing reports on the Monday debating whether this had been Torry's best game yet for Everton. His dazzling display was rewarded by scoring the third goal.

September also saw Everton launch their new club crest, which remains to this day. The motto read 'Nil Satis Nist Optimum', which translates as 'Only the Best is Good Enough', and the timing could hardly have been any more apt as the team on the pitch were shaping up as genuine contenders to be the best in the country.

The great start to the season came to an abrupt halt in spectacular fashion when Everton were thrashed 3-0 by bottom-of-the-table Huddersfield Town at Leeds Road. Bigger and soon to be life-changing matters unconnected to football were causing concern around the country and the teams were serenaded before kick-off by a rousing version of the national anthem. Prime minister Neville Chamberlain had been in Bad Godesberg – a borough of Bonn where foreign embassies were based at this time – to meet Hitler as he tried to avoid an escalation of events which could lead to war.

A week later, the ideal opportunity presented itself for Everton to wash away the memories of that chastening defeat at Huddersfield – a top-of-the-table Merseyside derby at Goodison. A crowd of 64,977 packed the terraces and stands and witnessed Everton triumph 2-1 with goals from Stan Bentham and Walter Boyes, with former Celtic player Willie Fagan replying for the Reds. Torry was described by the press as having been at his brightest and best during the match and 'the best forward on display'. His timing was impeccable and it was reported that he was favourite to start in the forthcoming Scotland international against Ireland. There were two extremely interested spectators in the stand on behalf of the SFA. One was called Bayley Martin and the other a certain Bill Struth.

Everton's form fluctuated a little after this and, after having won their first three away matches, it took until 4 December to win another, against Preston at Deepdale. Throughout this period, Gillick was consistently highlighted in the press reports for the high standard of his performances, typically being described as Everton's best attacker. It was also regularly noted that his consistent brilliance had coincided with being given a run in his more natural position on the right wing.

But just when the newspapers were full of articles on Everton being on the verge of completing a Football League record by having a 100 per cent home record in the first half of season, they suffered a serious hammering. A week before Christmas, they were routed 4-1 at Goodison by Charlton in a match where the final score could have been even worse. The one bright spot on a dark day was yet another fine Gillick performance, but this didn't stop the speculation over whether the team could handle the pressure at the top.

However, the Charlton defeat proved to be a blip, with the New Year seeing a return to form. The assault on the title was reignited with six straight wins, including a 3-0 derby win to stun a huge 56,000 crowd at Anfield. The match featured the sight of fans being helped out of the packed terraces by ambulancemen as the massive crowd swayed to the action. Fortunately, the worst reported injury was a broken leg. Two goals from Tommy Lawton helped the Toffees return to the top of the table on goal average ahead of Derby County. In tricky underfoot conditions, both Lawton's goals were created by Gillick. The first was a header from a Torry corner, the second a fine finish after a sublime though pass. All in all, a great day's work.

The *Liverpool Echo* report of the match heaped praise on Gillick's performance, describing one outrageous backheel as 'Meredithian', a comparison to the legendary Manchester United superstar Billy Meredith. The writer documented how sorry he felt for beleaguered Liverpool left-back Jim Harley, who was given the runaround by an unstoppable Gillick. The Everton wing wizard was said to have the beating of the defender 'with a mere flick of his boot'. Harley, who hailed from Fife, was one of the quickest defenders in English league football. He was so fast that he was a past winner of the famous Powderhall sprint race held every New Year in Edinburgh. His speed, however, was no match for the sheer talent of the winger he was trying to stop. The away fans at Anfield had enjoyed a Torry masterclass.

But again, just as the tide appeared to have turned for Everton, they suffered another astonishing defeat. This time the humbling was handed out by Wolves, who thrashed them a scarcely believable 7-0. Again, despite the scoreline, Gillick was reported as having had a fine match in which he repeatedly troubled the Wolves defence. Reports suggested Everton did not play particularly badly but that Wolves had simply been irresistible on the day. What a rollercoaster the Goodison fans were riding!

Despite this humiliation, Everton refused to be deflected from the race for the top prize and remained resolute, winning four out of the next five games, including wins at Elland Road and Old Trafford. Torry notched the second goal in the 2-0 win in Manchester, a match played before a surprisingly small crowd of 18,348. That victory over the red half of Manchester was a typical Gillick afternoon and one that led to a discussion which had raged in the press box being relayed to the Merseyside public in the *Liverpool Echo* on the Monday afterwards. The Everton reporter had overheard a Manchester-based colleague say after 20 minutes of play that he thought Gillick was lazy. The wiser head from the *Echo* wrote: 'He does not know his Gillick as we do. The Scot may appear to be lackadaisical, but watch him closely. He misses nothing.' Torry certainly didn't miss the Manchester United net when given the chance, which would undoubtedly have shut up the Old Trafford 'expert'.

That win put Everton five points clear at the top of table and the club's fifth league title was now within touching distance. Glory moved ever closer after the Easter fixtures when Gillick starred in three crucial victories in the space of just four days. The crammed holiday schedule started with a trip to Sunderland on Good Friday. The match was won 2-1, with all the goals coming in the first 20 minutes. The decisive strike saw Gillick knock home the rebound after his initial shot was saved by goalkeeper Albert Haywood.

In a run of fixtures that would terrify modern footballers, Everton then had to make the train journey down to the capital, with a visit to Chelsea just 24 hours later. More than 51,000 were packed into Stamford Bridge to see old Ibrox team-mates Stevenson and Gillick score a quickfire double in the second half to take the points to Goodison. Then, on Easter Monday, the team were back in action again in the reverse fixture with Sunderland. The Toffees were now in full flow and they swept aside the men from Roker Park 6-2. The goalscoring hero of the day was Stan Bentham, who hit a hat-trick, but the match report in the *Liverpool Post* made it clear who was the mastermind behind a victory that took the team to the verge of the championship. The writer stated: 'Gillick, in my opinion, is the best outside-right in any league.'

On 22 April 1939, Everton headed to The Valley to play Charlton Athletic knowing that one point would see them crowned champions. There was also the small matter of looking to avenge that terrible home defeat earlier in the season, with a championship party surely the perfect way to banish that memory. The result would not go the Toffees way, however, as they conceded in the first 30 seconds in a 2-1 defeat. But, with only remaining challengers Wolves dropping a point at Bolton, it meant the party was back on as Everton were now uncatchable. Despite a couple of unexpected beatings along the way, they were deserved title winners, with just two defeats after the turn of the year.

Torry had a prominent role on the decisive day, scoring Everton's goal after 60 minutes when he cleverly swept home a Joe Mercer cross. He was again singled out as the team's best attacker and was reported as having done everything possible to get the equaliser, with he and England international wing-half Mercer described as 'the masterminds trying to force a second'. The home campaign ended in typical Torry style when he was knocked out by Aston Villa goalkeeper Joe Rutherford in the act of heading the second goal in a 3-0 win. Remarkably, only 23,667 turned up to welcome home the champions. This was attributed to the live radio broadcast of the 1939 FA Cup Final between Portsmouth and Wolves, which the former won by 4-1. Gillick was able to finish the match, albeit having to constantly wipe blood off his face after taking Rutherford's fist clean on the nose. There was no question of him using the injury to duck out of a previously arranged benefit match against Northampton of the Third Division on the Monday. The decent crowd saw him score the first Everton goal in a 2-1 win, with the *Daily Post* saying he had shown the local fans 'the polish of First Division football'.

When the curtain came down on the competitive domestic season a week later, the 3-0 loss at Grimsby mattered little. Everton were acclaimed as worthy champions and had been lauded up and down the country for the quality of their football. Five points behind Derby in January, they finished 13 ahead of the Rams and four ahead of runners-up Wolves. They would be the longest-reigning champions in English football history, as this would prove to be the last full season for eight years due to the declaration of war in September 1939.

Torry's season was summarised by a joyful review of 1938/39 in the *Liverpool Echo*: 'While it took him a long time to produce his Rangers form, this season he has shown of what he is capable. It has often been said "Rangers do not let a good one go" but they let a good one go when they released Gillick. Since he became the recognised outside-right, he has played so well it is doubtful whether there is better. Some might plump for Matthews the juggler of football; I would prefer Gillick because he is a better team man. Matthews is without doubt a good worker of the ball, but the Scot gives more service to the team.' Given the magnificence of Stanley Matthews, this was quite the accolade and one that must have brought a broad smile of satisfaction to Torry's face.

A planned close-season tour of Germany to repeat the success of 1936 was inevitably cancelled considering the growing tensions in Europe and the menacing threat from Hitler. War was looking increasingly unavoidable and, less than a month into the new season, the inevitable happened. On 3 September 1939, Britain declared war on Germany, two days after Hitler had ordered the invasion of Poland. The announcement was made to the public in a radio broadcast by prime minister Neville Chamberlain at 11am that day. It was a day that would change the world forever and the impact on professional football was one small consequence to far bigger challenges facing the world.

The following day, the secretary of the Football League declared that football was to be suspended and all contracts with players were to be automatically cancelled as the country entered a time of national emergency. This was ratified in a proclamation from the Football Association on 8 September. It was decided that only friendly matches would be permitted in specific locations and on an amateur basis, with no payments to players permitted. The priority would be ensuring spectator and player safety before any match was given the green light.

On 14 September, the Home Office sanctioned the reopening of cinemas and theatres and, in turn, football grounds, so the prospect of competitive football seemed close again. Then, eight days later, strict conditions were set for the resumption of football, with the game to be organised in regional leagues. This set-up would continue until the Football League resumed in 1946/47.

Despite the civilian priorities in wartime Liverpool and despite the amateur nature of the football permitted, by the time the long dark days of winter arrived in November 1939, Torry had been subject to some serious criticism from a section of the Everton support who thought his displays lacked effort. However, he was to return to his spellbinding best on 11 November when he played a starring role in a 3-1 win against Manchester City. Gillick was reported as being the brightest player on the pitch, 'displaying brilliant work'. Due to the wartime situation, only 7,804 fans were present to see him in all his pomp, including netting the second goal.

Wednesday, 15 November 1939 was the day Gillick's time on Merseyside changed forever with the terrible garage fire at his Aintree home. After spending a number of weeks in hospital, during which he had a series of skin grafts, and a holiday in Scotland to recuperate, Gillick returned to the Blues side on 9 March 1940. This was after a couple of games as a guest in the Airdrie team who defeated Queen's Park in a two-legged Scottish Emergency War Cup first-round tie.

The following week, on 11 March, it was announced by club secretary Theo Kelly that Torry would not return to Everton until after the war. After his appearance against Manchester City, he had decided to return home before joining up with the services. He had tried to join up previously, but he had been exempt because of his injuries. He had been given a further three-month extension and, in the meantime, was expected to turn out for Airdrie. He gave up his home in Aintree and was planning to take up an aeroplane factory job while awaiting his call-up.

In the end, the wily Bill Struth persuaded Torry to return to his old stomping ground and, for the 1940/41 season, he was back in the Ibrox fold and this was where he largely remained until being officially transferred back to Rangers in December 1945. Perhaps the visit the Rangers manager had made back in 1938 when representing the SFA had played a part in the boss wanting his former player back. For all parties, it felt like a return home.

Gillick was a key player in the war years, helping Rangers win comfortably all the Southern League titles available and multiple cup competitions. The highlight was his hat-trick in the 8-1 trouncing of Celtic on New Year's Day 1943. While turning out as a guest player for Rangers during the war, there came a time when the player's registration would officially need to be resolved and Torry had made it clear he had no intention of returning to Merseyside.

In September 1945, both Torry and Jimmy Caskie turned out for the Toffees one last time. This came in the Lancashire Cup against Liverpool on 19 September 1945 when both travelled down from Scotland to play. Theo Kelly had contacted both men and was hopeful they would appear. It was initially reported that Torry could not make the match, but he arrived at Lime Street on the eve of the derby. He had hoped to appear the previous Saturday against Preston but could not arrange time off from work. It was a typically rip-roaring derby match which ended in a thrilling 3-3 draw after Everton were 3-0 ahead. Gillick wasn't a scorer, but one match report mentioned his 'facility for cannily slipping into scoring positions'. It was a game intelligence that the fans on the blue side of Merseyside were watching for the last time.

In the days following this match, negotiations commenced in earnest to secure the registrations of Gillick and Caskie. Around 23 October, Rangers opened with an offer of £3,000 for Torry or £5,000 for both. Hibs were hovering in the wings with a concrete interest in Caskie, who had been guesting for them during the war. Negotiations concluded on 21 November when both players were officially transferred to Ibrox and Torry's Merseyside adventure officially came to an end.

Gillick had been a registered Everton player for more than a decade and he had left a huge impression on Merseyside with team-mates and supporters. Many of those playing colleagues were happy to put their praise into print.

Gordon Watson, who played at half-back with Everton from 1933 to 1948, became great friends with Torry. He spoke of Gillick's initial homesickness, despite Liverpool being similar to Glasgow in many ways. Despite the presence of many Scottish players, such as Willie Miller, Jock Thomson, Jimmy Dunn and Jimmy Stein, Gillick found a close friend in Watson, a friendship that helped conquer his initial desire to return north.

Watson joked that 'as a rule, every great English club has a Scotsman in the team. But two can cause friction!' When club skipper Jock Thomson suffered an injury, Gillick became the only Scot to play regularly in that successful title run-in of 1939.

Torry Gillick medals from schools and junior football.

Central League title winners Petershill FC in 1933, with Torry in the front row.

Gillick with other Rangers youngsters David Kinnear and Jimmy Fiddes.

Torry playing for Rangers at Ibrox with Bob McPhail in the background, 1935.

Gillick in action for Everton.

Medal awarded after Stuttgart v Everton match in German tour of 1936.

Torry in Everton colours just after he signed.

Everton's league title-winning team of 1939 (great friend Gordon Watson is third from right in back row).

Gillick lines up for Scotland against Czechoslovakia in 1937.

Torry Gillick in his second spell at Ibrox after World War Two.

Torry drinks from the Scottish Cup after the 1948 final win over Morton.

Torry and Molly pictured at a team dinner in 1948.

Some of the different medals won by Torry Gillick at Rangers.

Torry takes to the field for his final club Partick Thistle alongside team-mate Jimmy McGowan.

Wedding picture of Torry and Molly from 30 December 1935.

Molly with baby Billy in 1936.

Youngest son Larry joins sisters Molly and Isobel for a treasured family picture.

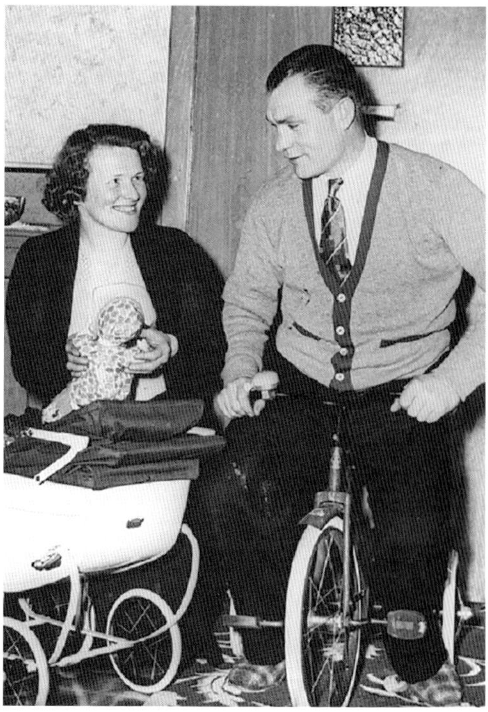

Molly and Torry are about to hide the kids' Christmas presents.

As a man, Watson described Gillick as 'a bright, confident and trustworthy friend who matured quickly at Everton. A good friend.' He also spoke highly of his friend's football ability. As a player, Watson described Gillick as 'fast, goal savvy and tricky – in that order. His primary mission was to cross the ball to centre-forwards Dixie Dean or Tommy Lawton; both were tremendous headers of the ball and prolific goal-getters. He was the main outlet for Cliff Britton's passes, an out-and-out touchline winger who was not expected to forage nor encouraged to defend.' Watson added: 'Torry was fast, but not as quick as an out-and-out sprinter like Albert Geldard [a winger who left shortly after Gillick arrived from Rangers]. Nonetheless, whenever he received the ball, Goodison held its collective breath. His control, plus a trick or two, enabled him to be versatile and adaptable. Although Torry boasted that he was two-footed, I think he favoured his right foot and preferred to play on the right wing.'

But it wasn't just his ability that Watson admired, it was also his dedication, durability and bravery. He talked of how the pair would stay behind after training to fire 40-yard passes at each other to hone their skills while the others had gone back into the dressing room to get a bath. As for bravery, Watson recalled: 'He would often play with more than just niggling ankle and hamstring injuries because he was fearful of surrendering his first-team spot. Trainer Harry Cooke would strap his ankles and rub iodine mixed with stray cigarette ash on the injured area; no magic spray in those days!'

He ended his tribute by pointing out the number of good wingers the club had on their books during Gillick's time at Goodison and making it clear who he saw as the best of them all: 'Torry had strong competition from other right and left-wingers during his time at Goodison. England's Wally Boyes, Ireland's Jackie Coulter, Ted Critchley, England's Albert Geldard and Harry Leyfield, as well as Doug Trentham to a lesser degree. He saw them all off.' Torry and wife Molly forged a lifelong bond with Gordon Watson and his wife, Olive, and they would visit each other in Liverpool and Scotland long after their playing days were over.

But it wasn't just Torry's lifelong friends paying tribute; many other Goodison stars queued up to praise the mercurial forward. Speaking in 1977, the great Dixie Dean described Jackie Coulter and Torry Gillick as 'two of the greatest wingers in the game'.

Tommy Jones was a Welsh defender who played more than 400 games for Everton and first saw Gillick when he was a schoolboy. Jones said that he was second only to Tommy Lawton as the fans' favourite. Jones would stand near the wall on the Goodison Road side and laughed when remembering how someone at the wall would ring a bell whenever Gillick started one of his dazzling dribbles to alert the crowd of impending entertainment.

Jones's observations were that Gillick was short and a bit lightweight and was initially hindered by the weight of his big transfer fee, but that he grew in confidence, especially after the arrival of Tommy Lawton (who in Jones's eyes was more effective, more athletic and a better all-round player than Dixie Dean). Gillick would knock the ball past his marker, then explode to catch it up and dribble with it under his complete control. Of course, he was subjected to some heavy tackles, but he never complained. Despite Gillick's starring role in the 1938/39 league title success, Jones felt Torry's best season was in 1936/37.

Stan Bentham was Gillick's unsung right-wing partner in the title-winning season. In an interview about that glorious campaign, Bentham remarked: 'It was my job was to run and challenge to get the ball and pass it to my right-winger who then won the hearts of the Goodison crowd.' He added: 'Sometimes Torry just stayed on the wing, seemingly not interested. But suddenly he'd tune in, go past three or four blokes as easy as anything, then either score or put over a great cross.' Bentham was another who mentioned Gillick's bravery and willingness to take the pain. He spoke of how team-mate Billy Cook 'tried to kick lumps off him' in training. Bentham pondered whether 'it could have been a Rangers-Celtic thing, except that Cook liked to bruise everyone'.

Renowned Everton historian David France, a great help in pulling together this section of the book, stated: 'My Evertonian father, who was a boxer and amateur footballer stationed in County Durham during the war, claimed to know a thing or two about the game [his best man was England's Raich Carter]. He described Gillick as "Tommy Ring with wings". In his eyes, Gillick was second to only "the Great Jackie Coulter" – that is how he referred to the

Irishman. He said that Gillick was an exciting winger with near-immaculate ball control, like Tommy Ring, Billy Bingham and Stanley Matthews.'

To be compared to some of the great wingers in English football is a great accolade and even more so when you consider Gillick was not an outright winger like the others but an all-round forward who could be equally brilliant at inside-forward and centre-forward.

France went on to say: 'I knew Torry was a brilliant, if mercurial, player, but reading the match reports from 1938/39 brought home to me that this was his annus mirabilis, when he found the consistency he had lacked previously. Prior to that, he had been tried in a few positions for Everton with mixed results, but got his wish in 1938/39 to be outside-right. He was integral to the title win.'

The respected historian added: "He was no traditional touchline hugger; he wandered infield, switching positions with fellow forwards, much to the bemusement of opponents. It helped that he played alongside great forwards like Tom Lawton and Alex Stevenson and had the tireless Stan Bentham doing donkey work for him. Who knows what he could have achieved in his peak years at Everton had the seven-year wartime hiatus not kicked in. And what a star he would have been in today's version of the game, ideal as a wide forward in a three or even as a second striker.' He ended his heartfelt tribute by speaking of Torry's loveable personality away from the pitch: 'He was game for a laugh, often conspiring with Stevenson and Boyes with tricks on team-mates. But it was not uncommon for him to be caught out by tricks played on him, which he took in the right spirit.'

Entertainer, personality, creator, goalscorer and league champion. Torry Gillick most certainly left his mark on the football players and the football public of Everton FC.

CHAPTER 6

THE DARK BLUE

AS THE 1936/37 season neared its end and Torry Gillick neared his 21st birthday, he could reflect on many great achievements already on the football field. A teenage winner of both the Scottish League and the Scottish Cup with Rangers, this had been followed by a successful big-money transfer to one of England's biggest clubs, where he was a virtually automatic choice. His second season at Goodison had not just consolidated him as an established top-flight player, he had also helped the club again retain their First Division status with a bit more to spare than the year before, even if 17th place wasn't where they wanted to be.

His 16 league and cup goals had proved his worth to his club and, on Wednesday, 21 April 1937, he was rewarded with a first call-up to the Scotland national team. Every professional player dreams of representing his country, and Gillick was no different. Here he was, at just 20 years of age, fulfilling yet another boyhood ambition. Scotland had just defeated England in front of the biggest-ever attendance at a football match, former Ibrox team-mate

Bob McPhail scoring twice in a 3-1 Hampden victory before an incredible 149,407 spectators. Gillick had been named as a reserve for the match but, in the days before substitutes, he was not required on the day. Now, though, he was to get his chance.

The national association had announced that the team would visit Austria and Czechoslovakia after the domestic season ended, with the selectors opting to make a few changes to the XI who had defeated the Auld Enemy. This was due to a combination of wishing to see fresh faces tried out in a friendly, plus a couple of regulars declaring themselves unavailable to travel. Among those ruling themselves out of the match in Vienna were McPhail and Derby County left-winger Douglas 'Dally' Duncan. The selectors decided the man to replace Duncan would be Torry Gillick.

There was one last Everton match to safely negotiate for Gillick, with his display in a meaningless last-day defeat to Grimsby being unusually quiet. Perhaps his mind was already on pulling the dark blue shirt over his head for the first time. The *Liverpool Echo* was certainly looking ahead, too, as it signed up Torry as its correspondent for the Scottish tour, with his thoughts on the matches to be printed back on Merseyside.

There was still a strong Ibrox presence in the travelling party, despite the fact old team-mate George Brown also pulled out of the first tour match because of his duties as a schoolteacher. Also on their way to Vienna were goalkeeper Jerry Dawson and team captain Jimmy Simpson, as well as former Rangers full-back Bert

Manderson, who was given the role of team trainer after impressing in this position with Queen's Park. The travelling party arrived in the Austrian capital by train, welcomed at the station by 10,000 people and the city band playing 'God Save the King'.

After their enthusiastic welcome, Scotland's reputation as being among the football elite was further illustrated by a record attendance of 62,000 cramming into the stadium for the match. Austria had been semi-finalists at the World Cup three years earlier and the public saw this match as a clash of two of the powerhouses of European football. As if a debut against one of the best teams in the world wasn't enough, Gillick then had to do the work of two men for most of the match. Scotland half-back Alex Massie suffered an injury in the opening minutes, resulting in him moving forward as Gillick's partner on the left side of attack while the selected inside-left Charlie Napier dropped back. With Massie hardly able to run, Gillick had to take on the challenge of breaking down the right side of the formidable Austrian defence on his own.

With only ten fit players, it was no surprise the relatively inexperienced Scots found themselves defending more often than attacking and Gillick's good friend Jerry Dawson showed why he had earned the 'Prince of Goalkeepers' nickname. It was a match where Gillick needed to show his teamwork and discipline more than his natural ability and he must have feared a debut defeat when the Austrians finally broke the Scottish resistance with just a quarter of an hour remaining. The huge crowd was silenced just moments later, however, when Preston's Frank O'Donnell scored a fine equaliser. The match ended 1-1, although there was one last injury scare when Gillick had to be carried from the field in the closing minutes after a bone-shaking collision with home defender Josef Pekarek. He was given a rousing cheer when limping back on to the park a few minutes later, determined to make sure his team held out.

The Scots were then due to travel to Czechoslovakia for a friendly in Prague, with a few more regular names joining up with the party. Following his injury, there was initially talk of him being allowed to leave the squad and join his Everton team-mates on their tour of Denmark, but he declared himself fit and, with Napier then ruled out of the match, it turned out that he was selected again after all. His new partner on the left needed little introduction as Gillick linked up with his old Ibrox colleague Bob McPhail in an attacking combination not seen for some time. With George Brown also back in the team alongside goalkeeper Dawson and skipper Simpson, Gillick had four good friends and trusted former team-mates lining up with him. Czechoslovakia were another excellent team, only losing the 1934 World Cup Final to Italy in extra time.

The match was played in sunshine and on a much better playing surface than in Vienna, and Gillick also shone brightly. Just four days away from his 21st birthday, he looked like a man destined for many more international honours. His clever footwork and interplay with McPhail gave the Czech defence a torrid time, with veteran home goalkeeper František Plánicka needing to be in inspired form to keep the rampant Scots out on the day he won a record 64th cap. One save, in particular, was breathtaking and it denied Gillick the first international goal that his play deserved.

The 35,000 crowd feared a goal had to come and, after 14 minutes, Scotland captain Jimmy Simpson scored it. After the Czechs fought back to equalise, the half-time score was given a more accurate reflection of the play when McPhail scored his seventh career goal in Scotland colours within a minute of that equaliser. Gillick had enjoyed much more of the ball in his second start in the dark blue and, despite not being on the scoresheet, he was a big part of Scotland's impressive forward play. He came close again after the interval when his free kick smashed off the crossbar with the goalkeeper beaten.

It wasn't much longer, however, before the name of Gillick was added to the list of players to score for Scotland. The young Everton forward took possession in the 73rd minute and rifled home a shot that even the hugely impressive Plánicka couldn't stop. He was mobbed by his team-mates who, as well as celebrating a goal that surely clinched victory, knew how much this goal meant to a popular colleague. The match finished 3-1, with Gillick receiving great reviews in the Scottish press for his performance. It looked like a long career in the dark blue was beginning.

In his report for the *Liverpool Echo*, a happy and proud Gillick wrote: 'The Czechs afterwards told us they had never seen football so good as the Scots played it. We have been banqueted and entertained all over this fine place. The Czechs are terribly kind. After the game there was a banquet, at which all the players received a pocket book, a purse, and a little copper plate with a footballer engraved. We left Prague on Sunday for Leipzig and were really sorry to go. I leave the Scottish party in Germany and go on to Copenhagen to join the Everton boys. It has been great being with the Scottish boys.' It seems somewhat surprising that Gillick then had to wait another year before being called up again. However, he suffered a bad knee injury during the annual Blues v Whites Everton trial match in August 1937 and was unable to return to action until mid-October. He may have returned too early, with niggling injuries and a struggle to rediscover his best form meaning there was little chance of an international return in the 1937/38 season. But things would improve dramatically the following season for both club and country.

Everton started the new season on fire, winning their first six league games to race to the top of the First Division table. Gillick was a key man in this impressive run and his form didn't go unnoticed by the Scotland selectors when they were deciding on a team to play against the Irish in Belfast in the opening match of the annual Home International Championship. He was chosen to start on the left wing, despite being ever-present on the other flank in Everton's explosive start. In a sign of a temporary shift in power domestically in Scotland, Gillick was joined by four Celtic players, with the only Ibrox representation being Jerry Dawson in goal. Gillick did have one other good friend on the pitch, though; his Goodison team-mate Alex Stevenson was in his regular Everton position inside left for the Irish.

The Scots were simply too strong for their hosts, with the 2-0 final scoreline summing up the difference in class. Gillick had an excellent match, time and again stretching the home defence with clever runs and probing passes. He came close to scoring, too, when a first-half shot thumped the crossbar. The goals were scored by Jimmy Delaney of Celtic and Tommy Walker of Hearts either side of half-time and Gillick would have been satisfied he had surely done enough to keep his place in the side next time. One reporter was sure he had impressed the selectors, stating: 'Gillick demonstrated footcraft, elusiveness and tactical knowledge of the highest order.'

Autumn 1938 was a tense time for the country, with Hitler's aggression on the Continent and the Munich Agreement he signed with prime minister Chamberlain making the front page headlines, but football provided an escape from the worries over another war and the next Home International match was scheduled just a month later, at home to Wales. It was no surprise when the selectors again named Gillick at outside-left, although there were a few changes to the XI, most notably a first cap for young Clyde goalkeeper John Brown in place of Dawson. There were three Hearts players in the team, perhaps partly due to the venue being Tynecastle rather than Hampden.

In the days before floodlights, a midweek match in early November meant an afternoon kick-off, but a crowd of almost

35,000 still travelled to Gorgie to watch the game. There had been a slight scare for Gillick the previous weekend when he limped off the pitch at Goodison after a win over Middlesbrough, but he was passed fit for the national team after reporting for duty. The Welsh had already beaten England in their opening match, so the winners here would be favourites to become the Home International champions and many in the press before the match were pessimistic of Scottish chances after some of the team had featured in a dismal loss in the annual league international against the English Football League the previous midweek.

It was to prove a memorable afternoon for Gillick, as he scored his first Scotland goal on home soil. The match didn't start too well, however, the Welsh taking the lead through Derby County centre-forward Dai Astley before 20 minutes had been played. But the Scots' superior teamwork and interplay started to tell and the equaliser arrived on the half-hour. Right-winger Jimmy Delaney of Celtic hared away from his full-back and sent over a wicked cross to the back post. The ball was met first time by incoming left-winger Gillick and the ball flew past Welsh goalkeeper Roy John before he could make any attempt to stop it. A marvellous goal that saw Gillick mobbed by his team-mates.

Despite this moment of brilliance, Gillick didn't enjoy the best of games, coming in for some criticism for some of his decision-making. The *Glasgow Herald* match report bemoaned him 'shooting from ridiculously acute angles'. However, even though he didn't perform at his brilliant best, Gillick did end up on the winning side for the third successive Scotland appearance. It ended 3-2, with Tommy Walker of Hearts grabbing two late goals before a Welsh consolation effort completed the scoring.

Perhaps Gillick's inconsistent display was explained on the Friday when Everton pronounced him doubtful for their weekend game, stating he had picked up an injury on international duty. Inconsistent or not, he now had the impressive record of two goals in four unbeaten appearances for his country. And he would soon be given the chance to add to that record, as Scotland had arranged a friendly against Hungary in early December, with the match to be played at his old Ibrox stomping ground.

Gillick would take to the Ibrox pitch with two current Rangers men in the national team, Jerry Dawson back in goal and future Rangers manager Scot Symon making his international debut at half-back. The 23,000 crowd certainly wasn't the biggest attendance any of them had played in front of at the stadium, but the small crowd saw an excellent first-half display from the home team. Gillick had come into the match on the back of a brilliant display against Chelsea the previous Saturday, his wing trickery given the accolade in the *Liverpool Echo* match report of having 'all the artifice of Matthews; in fact, more effective'. With the player in such fine form and his Everton team making a genuine title challenge, Gillick must have been a man brimming with confidence as he faced the team who had reached the World Cup Final just six months previously.

On a sodden pitch, and against a team who had decided to defend, Gillick gave a masterclass. One match report said the Everton winger was 'full of running and very tricky' and that the Hungarian defenders 'were at their wit's end trying to discover a means of stopping the former Rangers player'. Considering he was up against defenders who had starred at the World Cup, this was a truly special performance. In the first half, especially, Gillick tormented them time and again. By the interval, Scotland were three goals in front, with the Everton magician having a hand in every goal.

First, after 17 minutes, a sublime pass through to inside-forward Andy Black saw the Hearts man chopped down before he could shoot. His Tynecastle team-mate Tommy Walker scored from the spot. Just eight minutes later came the most memorable moment of the match. Gillick seemed to be surrounded by Hungarian defenders out on the wing but, with a sudden backheel and change of direction, he made space to fire over a dangerous cross which eventually fell at the feet of Black, who hammered it into the net. Then, with half an hour not yet on the clock, Gillick took advantage of hesitancy in the bedraggled visiting defence to nip in between goalkeeper and a defender to blast the ball home.

It looked like a hammering was on the cards, but Gillick's inside-forward partner Black was forced to limp off the pitch before half-time meaning Scotland would play with ten men in the second half. The game's most dangerous player in the opening period now had the job of two players to do. Unsurprisingly, this prevented

Gillick, and Scotland, from dominating proceedings. The only goal of the second period would come at the other end when the Hungarians were awarded a late penalty. Still, Gillick's unbeaten record continued and he looked set for a glorious international career. As things turned out, this would actually be his fifth and final official cap for his country.

The following April, the Scottish selectors incredibly decided to name him only as a reserve for the annual clash with England despite his great form for Everton helping push them to the brink of the league title. The selectors decided on Middlesbrough's Jackie Milne as left-winger for the big match, despite him also playing on the right wing for his club. One Glasgow journalist pondered whether the relatively untried Milne would 'bring to the attack the shrewdness and cunning of Gillick'. The 149,000 Hampden crowd got the answer to that question when the English came from behind to win 2-1. The hapless Milne was the target of much criticism from fans and in the press. The *Glasgow Herald* stated the player demonstrated he was 'the left winger with no left foot', although most of the writer's displeasure was aimed at the selectors rather than the player. It seemed that Gillick's absence had actually made his value to the Scotland team all the more obvious. Sadly, with war declared a few months later, there would be no more official caps awarded for nearly seven years.

There were, however, unofficial wartime matches played between national sides, albeit often in strange circumstances and sometimes with relatively makeshift line-ups. The first England v Scotland match during the conflict was a case in point, with the match played at Newcastle and England limited to selecting only northern-based players due to travel restrictions. To add to the slightly surreal occasion, a car taking two of the England players to the match was involved in an accident. This forced their last-minute withdrawal and England fielded two Newcastle United players who had been in the crowd as spectators. One of them was Tommy Pearson, a Scottish winger who would be selected for his own country in a later wartime international! Incredibly, the Scots still lost the match 2-1.

Gillick was unavailable for this encounter due to the injuries he sustained in the fire at his Merseyside home, but by May 1941 he had returned to Rangers and was in great goalscoring form when the selectors were deciding who to pick for the Hampden visit of the English. They decided he was the man to play on the right wing and that he would have Ibrox team-mates Jerry Dawson, Jock Shaw, Jimmy Smith and Alex Venters in the team with him. Another familiar face was his former Everton colleague Jimmy Caskie on the left wing; he was now temporarily playing for St Mirren and would one day join up at Rangers, too.

Despite the strong Ibrox presence and despite the noisy backing of 78,000 fans desperate for some wartime cheer, Gillick found himself enduring something of a beating. Venters gave the Scots a first-half lead, but the English were simply too powerful, with another old Everton team-mate Joe Mercer outstanding. The match ended 3-1 to the visitors and, in truth, this didn't reflect the gulf between the teams on the day. The English had an exceptional generation of players, with legendary names such as Stanley Matthews, Stan Cullis, Denis Compton and Wilf Mannion earning the grudging admiration of the Hampden masses.

Gillick would play twice more against England during the war in these unofficial matches and the results got progressively worse. The teams played each other twice or three times a year, with the matches seen as morale boosters for the public and a means of raising funds to support the war effort. Team selection greatly depended on availability, with players often unavailable because they were either employed in essential domestic jobs or serving in the forces. Gillick's next appearance was a great example, the match this time played at Wembley in January 1942, the second meeting within a matter of months under the Twin Towers. The proceeds for this match went to the Red Cross to Russia Fund, and Winston Churchill's wife, Clementine, gave a speech before kick-off to the 64,000 spectators.

In another miserable experience for Gillick, he saw his team go a goal down within the first minute, then saw his old friend and Goodison team-mate Tommy Lawton add two more. To complete the agony, he was carried from the field near the end after colliding heavily with English goalkeeper George Marks and was unable to return to the fray. If he was to think this would be his lowest day in the dark blue, Gillick was to suffer even greater heartache in

October 1943 when he made his third and final wartime appearance against England.

The year had started with him making history at club level, his hat-trick helping Rangers to an 8-1 win over Celtic on New Year's Day – still the biggest competitive win in the fixture – but ten months later he would trudge off the pitch at Maine Road, Manchester, as part of a Scotland team handed their biggest-ever defeat in front of 60,000 delighted English fans.

England were handing Scotland regular beatings; the last match between the teams in April had been a 4-0 thumping at Hampden. The Scottish selectors, with several experienced men missing and seemingly little to lose, opted to field an experimental XI featuring five international debutants in goalkeeper Joe Crozier of Brentford, Adam Little of Rangers, Willie Campbell of Morton, and St Mirren pair Alex Linwood and John Deakin. There was also just a second Scotland start for George Young and a fourth appearance for Willie Waddell. Both were young players of enormous promise, but so many novices in the line-up was a suicidal approach against a team of exceptional ability. Gillick was one of the few older heads in the team, but he was powerless to prevent a massacre.

The Scots managed to hold out for 14 minutes but, once Sheffield United's Jimmy Hagan opened the scoring, it was a case of how many England would score. One match report summed up the chasm between the teams by saying England possessed too much experience, craft, pace and physique. That was reflected in a rapidly worsening scoreline. After a chastening 45 minutes which saw Gillick and his team-mates chasing shadows, the Scots left the pitch already 5-0 behind, with Tommy Lawton completing a hat-trick. By the end, the home crowd were sympathetically cheering any positive Scottish play in the hope of seeing some competitive action, but the three remaining goals were all scored into the Scotland net. Lawton ended up with four, England with eight. The last goal was scored by Stanley Matthews, a player who had played alongside Gillick in Rangers colours as a guest during these unique times.

Gillick was spared any more humiliation, this being his last appearance in the full Scotland team, so he mercifully missed five more wartime defeats handed out by a genuinely great England team. Three of these games saw the English score six times, with the 6-1 win at Hampden in April 1945 the biggest-ever home loss suffered by the Scots. Maybe it's just as well that all these wartime matches were unofficial and the results not included in the record books! That means that the Scottish FA has Gillick's international record as five undefeated appearances, with three goals scored.

After the war finally ended and Gillick had made his move back to Rangers permanent, he was never chosen for the full international team. But he did wear the dark blue three times in these successful twilight years of his Ibrox career. These were all in league international matches, which were a popular and competitive part of the football calendar. His first match in Scotland colours came in April 1947 at Windsor Park in Belfast and the match between the Irish and Scottish league teams produced even more goals than that Maine Road drubbing. It ended 7-4 to the Scots, with Airdrie forward Bobby Flavell scoring five times. But the goal of the game, and the defining moment in a titanic tussle, was provided by Gillick.

With the scores level at 4-4 and the clock showing less than 20 minutes remaining, he took possession out wide, cut inside two defenders, then unleashed an unstoppable shot from all of 25 yards that was past goalkeeper Smyth before he could move. In a Scottish team that included many of the best players in the country, such as Willie Woodburn and Jock Shaw of Rangers and Willie Ormond of Hibs, it was the wily veteran who gave the 20,000 crowd the biggest moment of magic.

Early 1948 saw his other two league international appearances, with his next start also against the Irish, with the venue this time being Parkhead in mid-January. In a sign of the huge popularity of football in post-war Scotland, just over 50,000 fans attended the match, which the Scots were expected to win easily. But again it was something of a struggle until Gillick stepped in. The home crowd were getting increasingly nervy as the Irish mounted a late rally after going a goal behind in the first half. Then, with just eight minutes remaining, Gillick provided an inch-perfect through ball for centre-forward Billy Houliston to score his second goal of the game. A late third goal completed the scoring, the 3-0 final score flattering the Scots somewhat.

Two months later, Gillick wore the Scotland colours for the final time. Now approaching his 32nd birthday, he was selected alongside Sammy Cox and George Young to face the Football League at St James' Park in Newcastle on St Patrick's Day. This swansong in dark blue was perhaps better remembered for events off the pitch than on it.

The match itself ended in a 1-1 draw, the great Blackpool forward Stan Mortensen putting the English in front before a late penalty by Young won the Scots a share of the spoils. Gillick had a fine match, with some newspapers speculating that he might be due a recall to the full team for the next international. The team went back to their hotel, the journey back north having been arranged for the following morning after breakfast. This would become the most famous meal Gillick ever ate.

The year 1948 was a time of rationing and austerity, with Britain trying to rebuild after the massive losses and expenditure of wartime. The team were instructed by their management that the Scottish League and SFA were in a period of great financial constraints and that any meals taken should be the minimum to avoid unnecessary spending. This meant that, after their exertions the previous evening, the team were expected to make do with a light breakfast to tide them over until they got home. The players reluctantly followed instructions and were, no doubt, still hungry after their meagre meal. All players, that is, with one notable exception.

Torry Gillick decided to order the full English and his team-mates looked on enviously as he tucked in. He told the hotel that the bill should be sent to the Scottish League. The football authorities, on receiving the hotel bill, were less than happy. Rangers were contacted and told they should be the ones to stump up for their player's extravagant spending. Manager William Struth responded – but not in the way the League bosses expected. His return letter contained the original hotel bill along with a short but simple message. He wrote that Rangers players were always treated to the best when representing the club and that they must be treated the same way when representing their country. If the authorities could not afford to treat his players properly, then he would recommend they stop selecting players from Ibrox.

Rangers never did pay the bill. Struth had shown yet again his unbending philosophy of what was right for his players and it can only be presumed the governing body settled the account after all. One can only speculate whether this was a reason why Gillick never represented Scotland at any level again. It was an international career in which he played alongside and against some of the best players in the world at the time and he provided goals, skill and memorable moments on the highest stage. There were impressive wins and there were terrible defeats. His official record of five caps and three goals certainly doesn't tell the full story.

CHAPTER 7
THE WAR YEARS

WHEN BRITAIN declared war on Germany on 3 September 1939, the face of football underwent a drastic change. Only five games had been played in the Scottish top flight when the season was suspended. Following ongoing discussions between the relevant authorities, it was eventually agreed at a meeting on 15 September 1939 that competitive football could resume on a regional basis. Rangers would go on to win the 1939/40 Western Division title, then beat Eastern Division champions Falkirk in a play-off to determine the overall league winners.

By the 1940/41 season, the format had been altered, although not as the Scottish League had hoped. In the summer of 1940, it was proposed that the system of promotion and relegation between the first and second divisions should resume. This did not materialise, but the western and eastern set-up was altered to a different regional format of southern and northern divisions.

In early 1940, Torry had returned to Scotland to rehabilitate after the burns he suffered in that terrible Merseyside garage incident. For a time, his football career hung in the balance. Due to his injuries and a willingness to help the war effort, Torry and his wife, Molly, made the decision to return to more familiar territory and, once back in Scotland, Gillick took on a job at an aeroplane factory while also signing up as a reservist for the RAF.

Once fit enough to play again, he appeared as a guest for his home town team of Airdrie. Initially during wartime football, the Scottish football authorities permitted clubs to maintain a £2-per-week wage for players, which was more than their English counterparts. With income tax on all earnings significantly increased to raise extra funds for the war effort, it meant a number of star players based down south headed north to play as guests when their wartime commitments allowed. There were numerous examples of famous players turning out for both the larger and less fashionable Scottish clubs. Matt Busby at Hibs, Bill Shankly at Partick Thistle and Tommy Lawton at Morton were three of the best known, along with the wonderful winger Stanley Matthews, who made two appearances for Rangers and also turned out for Airdrie and Morton.

As well as Lawton, another Goodison team-mate of Gillick's travelled north to become a guest player in the Scottish game. Winger Jimmy Caskie chose St Mirren and then Hibs as his temporary football homes, although he would be wearing the blue of Rangers by the time wartime competition ended.

Gillick turned out ten times in total for Airdrie, with six of these appearances coming in the Western League, which was eventually won by Rangers. He missed out on playing for the opposition at Ibrox, however, as Airdrie's visit there in mid-February had been the week before his debut for the Diamonds. He scored once in those league appearances and added three more goals in his four starts in the Emergency War Cup, a tournament that only took place in the 1939/40 season. One of those goals was on his Airdrie debut against Queen's Park. He actually made 11 appearances, but a cup replay at Tynecastle was abandoned after 116 minutes with the scores level at 2-2 due to darkness, with the referee and players no longer able to see the ball!

After his short spell at Airdrie, Torry played two trial matches in the summer of 1940, one for Partick Thistle and one for Rangers. He was paid the princely sum of £2 each time, something that Gillick in later years would remark had made him feel like a millionaire at a time of harsh austerity. When it came to a choice of clubs, it was obvious which of the Glasgow sides would win his signature. Rangers manager William Struth prevailed, of course, and Gillick's signature was rewarded with a generous £20 signing-on fee. He was back with his first love, the club he never really wanted to leave in the first place. On hearing about the signing-on fee, Torry was quoted as saying: 'I did not feel I was a millionaire that day, I knew I was one.' Among the many milestones and honours Torry received during his career, it is perhaps the greatest accolade that he was the only player signed twice by arguably the most influential figure in Rangers' entire history, manager Struth.

Some were possibly surprised that Struth brought the player back. There could be no denying that Gillick's carefree maverick attitude on and off the pitch was the antithesis of Struth's public reputation as a strict disciplinarian. Gillick, though, was without any shadow of doubt one his favourite 'boys', as he liked to describe the players under his charge.

Everyone involved, from players and officials to spectators, had to adjust to the altered conditions, but they had the wholehearted backing of a government which believed football should continue as a distraction to the stressful times the population were enduring. There would be competition, but under special conditions. All honours won, appearances made and goals scored are not officially recognised due to the unofficial nature of these competitions. But these were still competitive games and, official or not, they are part of football history and should be remembered. And, despite the circumstances, there were many memorable football occasions on which Gillick was able to shine.

The main national domestic competitions pre-war, the league and Scottish Cup, were put into cold storage. The league was replaced initially with the Regional Scottish War Emergency League and the Scottish Cup by the War Emergency Cup. Both of these competitions lasted just one season and both were won by Rangers. When Gillick made his second Rangers bow in August 1940, the league set-up now saw Rangers compete in the Southern League, with a North Eastern League for clubs in that region. There would be no national cup competition; instead, Rangers would compete in the Southern League Cup, a wartime forerunner to the Scottish League Cup introduced after the war.

The football season was also extended into the summer to maintain the distraction of attending sporting events available to the Scottish public. A Summer Cup competition was introduced, although Rangers did not compete in it in every season of its existence.

In later years, Rangers captain Jock 'Tiger' Shaw offered his view about the war years. He said, 'I think standards did decline during the war years because teams were forced to field guest players or their own lads, home from leave, or even laddies too young to join up. We were quite fortunate. Willie Thornton was stationed in England and played several games for teams down there, but players such as Willie Waddell, Andy Cheyne and George Jenkins all had engineering backgrounds and were put to work in the local shipyards so they could still play for Rangers. As far as I am aware, we never struggled for players.' They never struggled for players and they certainly never struggled to win trophies. Struth's team dominated these temporary tournaments, giving Gillick the opportunity to play in many more finals and to pick up plenty of medals.

Torry's first appearance second time around came in the Southern League season of 1940/41 on 10 August at Brockville, scoring the third goal in a 3-1 win before 12,000 spectators. He lined up in his new and regular position of inside-right and was alongside just three men who had started on his last competitive appearance for the club almost five years earlier at Perth. Goalkeeper Jerry Dawson, right-back Dougie Gray and centre-forward Jimmy Smith were the men who shared the pitch with him on both occasions.

Rangers played in unfamiliar hooped shirts and got off to a terrible start. Falkirk – who had won the Eastern Division the previous season but lost the play-off final to Rangers – clearly had revenge in mind and Rangers had goalkeeper Dawson to thank in the early stages for keeping the home forwards at bay. But the inevitable happened in the 17th minute when former Celtic forward Charlie Napier sidestepped a Willie Woodburn challenge before firing the Bairns ahead.

Only a last-ditch goalline clearance by Dougie Gray prevented Falkirk going two ahead. When you also consider Falkirk hit the woodwork three times in the first half, it shows how dominant they were, but somehow Rangers reached the interval only one behind. Gillick's reintroduction to the Rangers team was not going as planned.

The second half started in the same vein, with the home side swarming around the Rangers goal and Dawson coming to Rangers' rescue yet again with a fine diving save from winger Carruthers after his shot looked destined for the bottom corner. That save, though, appeared to dishearten Falkirk and, in the 55th minute, Rangers capitalised on some slack marking. Centre-forward Jimmy Smith, with his back to goal, managed to hook the ball high past keeper

McKie for the equaliser and the momentum shifted significantly. Smith had also scored in Gillick's last Rangers appearance in December 1935, and the bustling big centre-forward had regularly hit the opposition net in the intervening years while Torry was down south.

In an attempt to regain their earlier superiority, the home side switched centre-forward and right-winger. This backfired, as Marshall had been causing Rangers all sorts of problems on the right and the switch nullified that threat. Rangers went on to capitalise. Left-winger Charlie Johnston won a 50-50 race for the ball with the home goalkeeper and dispatched the ball into the empty net. Rangers then tightened their grip on the game, hitting both the crossbar and post twice and having what looked like a perfectly good goal disallowed.

Then, with six minutes remaining, the points were secured with a goal from the man making his second Rangers debut. Gillick lashed a vicious shot high into the Falkirk net after some brilliant interplay between him and right-wing partner Willie Waddell. This would be the first of countless days where the pair's almost telepathic understanding helped Rangers rip apart defences and win matches.

The Gillick-Waddell partnership was one based on great respect for each other's individual ability, but also on the fact both men had a wicked sense of humour and enjoyed trying to get one over on the other. They would sometimes appear to be fighting like cat and dog on the pitch, both men having the highest expectations of the other, given their ability. But this seemingly confrontational relationship could not have been further from the truth. The two men who formed one of the greatest right-wing partnerships ever seen in Scottish football became the closest of friends, right up until Gillick's death.

Waddell would sometimes look frustrated if he thought Torry had overhit a pass to him, once complaining that 'Gillick thought he had a hare on the right touchline'. But these Gillick passes were often judged perfectly into open space to utilise Waddell's lightning pace and wonderful crossing ability, with many a Rangers goal starting with one of their combinations. Gillick, in return, would moan that Waddell would make him sprint unnecessarily when a simpler pass was on, stating that the 'master of the ball' shouldn't be asked to sprint for it.

Years later, in an article in the *Evening Times*, Waddell reminisced about his lasting friendship with Torry and told a story of how he one day accused Gillick of trying to kill him! He had taken his family north on a holiday and, quite by chance, bumped into his old Ibrox team-mate as he was setting off on one of his regular fishing trips. When Waddell remarked that he didn't understand what pleasure a man could get from standing in cold water waiting in vain for a fish to appear, Torry instantly offered him a spare rod and promised to give Willie a day to remember.

After they arrived at a fast-flowing river, Torry showed his friend how to cast a line and the best spot to stand so he would hook a salmon. That best spot was standing on a small rock right in the middle of the river. The inevitable happened. Waddell cast his line, the stone moved under his feet and into the water he went. As well as having to haul himself out of the freezing water, he had gashed his leg on a sharp surface of the very rock Torry had told him was safe.

Waddell carried the scar on his leg for the rest of his days and obviously wasn't going to let his friend forget about it. He told the newspaper reporter: 'That little so and so. He used to try to kill me on the field and here he was now trying to murder me by drowning!' But these adventures together were in the future and it was a future that started with the pair sharing in a highly successful first season together in the Rangers team. Torry's goalscoring start continued, hitting the opposition net in each of the first four league matches, including twice in a 5-1 win over Hibs which also saw a double from a youngster called Ian McPherson. These would be the last league goals McPherson scored for the club; he enlisted with the RAF shortly afterwards and became a highly decorated and successful pilot of Mosquito fighter bombers. After the war ended, the Scot decided to stay down south, where he won the English First Division title with Arsenal.

Gillick missed the first final of the season, when Celtic surprised Rangers in the Glasgow Cup. But a first wartime winner's medal was merely delayed. He started in 22 of the 30 Southern League fixtures, with Rangers ending a hard-fought season as champions by just three points from Clyde. A 3-0 win over the Shawfield men in mid-February had been crucial on the way to the championship, Gillick giving an outstanding display which included a wonderful goal. The inaugural Southern League Cup was then won to give the club another wartime double, Gillick scoring in wins over Falkirk, Third Lanark and Dumbarton in the early rounds before playing his part in a replayed final victory over Hearts, which Rangers won 4-2 in front of more than 60,000 fans thanks to two goals in the final five minutes.

Just a fortnight later, Rangers reached the final of the Glasgow Charity Cup, with the match against Partick Thistle making headlines when it became known that the great English winger Stanley Matthews would be guesting for Rangers. He had played once before for Struth's men, in a league match against Morton the previous season, and many in the 30,000 crowd went along to see the great man in action. But it was a star from closer to home who stole the show.

The Hampden crowd saw a Matthews who clearly wasn't fit and who contributed little. They also saw Rangers win 3-0 and Torry Gillick score twice in a display that the legendary Englishman would have been proud of. The almost never-ending season was then completed by the Summer Cup competition. Gillick again scored in the final but his third-minute opener wasn't enough as Hibs came back to claim a 3-2 win on 12 July 1941, the season ending a full 11 months after it had started.

In amongst all these competitions, the team also played a number of benefit matches to aid those impacted by the horrors of war. There were a couple of examples of these in 1941. Firstly, in April, Rangers took on a select team representing the RAF to raise funds for the Clydebank Air Distress Fund after the town suffered horrific damage and heavy casualties during the blitz. Then, in September, Rangers defeated Preston North End 3-1 in a match organised to raise money for the Glasgow War Fund. Gillick scored the second Rangers goal and the occasion was marked by the presentation to the winners of the Bruce Casket, a replica of the one in which the heart of Robert the Bruce had been transported back to Scotland from Spain many centuries earlier. The casket became a display item in the Ibrox trophy room.

With three trophies won in his first season back, Gillick must have been looking forward to the 1941/42 season despite having had hardly any rest from the previous campaign. The first Southern League match was played on 9 August, just four weeks after the 1940/41 season concluded with that Hibs defeat. If Torry was feeling tired, he didn't show it, scoring in a comfortable 3-0 win over Motherwell. The new season would be a prolific one for Gillick, who scored often and scored important goals into the bargain.

At the end of August, he scored his first hat-trick back in Rangers colours in a 6-1 demolition of Airdrie. The following weekend, on 6 September, he scored in a controversial Old Firm match which made headlines. It was reported that incredible scenes were witnessed before kick-off when the Irish tricolour was waved during the playing of the national anthem, this during the darkest days of the war when the Irish republic remained neutral in the fight against Nazi Germany.

Rangers were well in command approaching the interval, 2-0 ahead thanks to an Alex Beattie goal and Torry's first against the 'old enemy' since his return. The game then erupted with the award of a penalty to Celtic following a foul by Jerry Dawson on Jimmy Delaney. Rangers players protested at length to referee Willie Webb and, when Frank Murphy's penalty was saved, the Celtic supporters behind Dawson's goal reacted furiously. A cascade of bottles rained down, with some players seeking refuge by standing in the nets.

When order was restored, the Ibrox men eventually triumphed 3-0, Alex Venters hitting the final goal. By then, Celtic were reduced to nine fit men after Crum and Delaney were injured. Celtic Park was closed for one month by the SFA as punishment for the unsavoury scenes, provoking a protest by the Roman Catholic newspapers in the city and an outburst from Provost Patrick Dollan who raged: 'This judgement is more like Nazi policy than British fair play.'

The first cup competition of the new season was the Glasgow Cup and, after their recent explosive encounter, it was inevitable the Old Firm would draw each other in the semi-final. The football authorities took no chances of the trouble being repeated, limiting the Hampden attendance to just 15,000 and keeping a large 'no-man's land' between the two sets of fans. In another amazing match, there were four penalties awarded. Rangers scored from the only one they were awarded, while Celtic saw Jerry Dawson save two of their attempts. Those misses proved costly, Rangers winning 3-2, with Gillick netting what proved to be the winner.

He also hit the net in the final, a one-sided affair against Clyde in which Rangers cantered to a 6-0 victory. This final also saw another guest player in blue, Manchester City's Les McDowall filling Gillick's usual position of inside-right while Torry played through the middle. McDowall would go on to fame as the manager of City when they lifted the 1956 FA Cup, a match made famous when their German goalkeeper Bert Trautmann played on after suffering a broken neck. He was also famous for introducing the deep-lying centre-forward tactic into the English game, a position occupied by Don Revie in his City team.

In the league, Rangers' dominance was being challenged by a strong Hearts team and, when the sides met at Ibrox in November 1941, they were locked together at the top of the table on 22 points apiece. It was billed as a vital match for both sides and an attendance of around 30,000 saw a classic encounter that lived up to the hype.

It was to be a match in which two players stole the show, the respective inside-rights, Gillick and Tommy Walker. Their skills did much to give the Ibrox crowd a memorable afternoon's football. With just four minutes played, the fans had already seen two moments of brilliance, with each side getting on to the scoresheet. The scorers of the goals were Messrs Gillick and Walker.

The Hearts man put his side in front when he capitalised on good work by inside-left Alex McCrae and beat Rangers deputy goalkeeper George Jenkins with a fierce shot from just around the penalty spot, bringing grimaces to the Ibrox faithful. But if the visitors thought they were on their way to a rare Ibrox victory, they were soon to realise the folly of such thinking. A minute later, Gillick picked up the ball some 25 yards from goal, took two paces forward and unleashed a rocket of a shot which almost demolished the goalpost before flying into the net.

That set the scene for the day's entertainment, both sides playing wonderful attacking football and, in the early stages, Hearts looked the likely winners as they swept aside Rangers with Walker playing a pivotal role in the Jambos' forward thrusts. There were several near things in the Rangers goalmouth with the Light Blues having good cause to be thankful to goalkeeper Jenkins on more than one occasion.

Jenkins covered himself in glory in the 20th minute when McCrae barged through the Rangers defence and fired in a powerful shot which appeared destined for the roof of the net until Jenkins leapt to touch the ball on to the crossbar. The danger was still there as the ball rebounded from the bar into the path of the onrushing Tommy Adams, but Jenkins threw himself at the Hearts man's feet and smothered the effort, to the cheers of the fans.

Hearts were to pay dearly for their failure to capitalise on the chances they created. In a five-minute spell near the end of the first half, Rangers struck with a vengeance, scoring three goals in quick succession to sink Hearts' table-topping aspirations.

The first of the trio was scored by Jimmy Smith, who outjumped centre-half Jimmy Dykes to nod a Charlie Johnston cross into the postage stamp corner of the net. Three minutes later, Gillick again showed the power of his shooting, cracking the ball home from outside the penalty area. With Hearts now reeling, Gillick sent Willie McIntosh clear on the right and the winger sent a superb cross to the far post where Johnston raced in to make it four.

To Hearts' credit they continued to fight but, with their tails up, the Ibrox men had no intention of conceding their advantage and the visitors' cause looked hopeless. Tommy Walker did get his name on the scoresheet again when he crashed a Jackie Gillies cross past Jenkins from ten yards out and there were flickering signs of a Hearts fightback as the Edinburgh men tried to repeat Walker's effort.

However, with full-backs Jock and Dougie Gray, along with centre-half George Thomson, on top form, Hearts were banging their heads against a brick wall, particularly with goalkeeper Jenkins emulating his defenders. It must have been frustrating for the Hearts players because, make no mistake about it, they were playing well and were matching Rangers in every department of the game except where it mattered most, in front of goal.

Rangers proved that point four minutes from time when the McIntosh-Johnston combination which had produced the fourth goal reversed roles to net the fifth, McIntosh heading a Johnston cross past the diving Anderson. Rangers had run out convincing winners, but there was no lack of sympathy for Hearts, who had met the Ibrox men on a day when a player of the calibre of Gillick was at his best.

Torry was the man who had made Rangers tick that day, spraying passes to both wingers and serving up shooting of an accuracy and power second to none. Only he could have overshadowed an in-form Tommy Walker in the way he did and, considering Walker had been the first-choice Scotland international inside-right for several years, it was a clear demonstration of the wonderful talent Gillick possessed.

Having opened a two-point gap by virtue of that 5-2 win, Rangers held on to their place at the top to register yet another title win, maintaining their iron grip on wartime silverware. Hearts faded after their Ibrox loss, with Edinburgh rivals Hibs finishing runners-up, albeit a distant eight points behind the champions. Gillick played in 24 of the 30 Southern League matches, hitting the net an impressive 20 times. One of those appearances was an astonishing 8-1 defeat at Easter Road, a result that nobody could have ever imagined and which showed the unpredictable nature of a highly competitive Scottish football scene. Alex Venters was sent off during the match, a rare occurrence in football in the 1940s, but there were no excuses offered from manager Struth, who congratulated his Edinburgh rivals on a devastating performance. It seems incredible that, during the war, when Gillick played in so many great victories, he would suffer two eight-goal reverses – one each for club and country.

The Southern League Cup was also retained, with Gillick's goals again a major influence. He hit seven goals in six group-stage matches, including vital winners home and away against Hearts. Winning the group set up a semi-final with Celtic. He didn't score in the 2-0 win at Ibrox, but he was instrumental in all that was good in the Rangers attack on a day when Alex Venters and Charlie Johnston scored the goals. Morton awaited in the final on Saturday, 9 May 1942 at Hampden, an occasion that attracted almost 45,000 spectators. In a tight match where the underdogs gave Rangers much to think about, it was that man Gillick who made the difference, scoring the only goal of the match in the 28th minute.

In the Morton side that day was a teenage inside-left who would go on to become one of Scotland's finest players in the post-war years, Billy Steel. When Torry hung up his boots in the early 1950s, Steel recalled both that Southern League Cup Final and also what it was like to share a pitch, and occasionally a dressing room, with the irrepressible Gillick. In a press interview, Steel said, 'Torry played for Rangers against Morton during the war many times and I used to enjoy the tussles between him and Jimmy Whyte, the hardman of the Cappielow bunch. The great games he has played will be remembered by football fans all over Scotland, but I sometimes feel that Torry's greatest displays were reserved for training days when players get the ball out for a kickabout. It is on these occasions that he really gets to it with impersonations of such things as desperate dives by goalkeepers, goalscoring headers or shots and all manner of dashing deeds which footballers execute during the fray. His comic ridicule is something other players enjoy. They recognise how funny it is to see themselves in their most serious moments.' He went on 'The Gillick goal I will most remember was a shot from his right foot in the 1942 League Cup Final between Rangers and Morton at Hampden. It was a very hard game and both Billy Campbell and Jimmy Whyte, our wing-halves, were doing a lot better than average. We were holding our own and, in the early part of that game, looking most likely to score. Willie Waddell then got the ball, beating Andy Fyfe on the corner flag, and made his way to the byeline. Gillick timed his approach perfectly, getting the ball from Waddell and, without stopping it, let go from the edge of the box and our goalkeeper Archie McFeat didn't see the ball until he turned round to pick it out his net. He scored many and made a lot more but, to me, Torry is at his best in his character parts behind the goal. I am sure he could get a job on stage when his football days are over.'

Three trophies had now been won, with the Charity and Summer cups still available. Holders Rangers reached the first final, with Clyde the team looking to stop the next leg of a clean sweep. Gillick started at centre-forward and was instrumental in Rangers dominating play in the first 20 minutes. It looked a matter of time before Rangers scored, but he then suffered a muscle injury that forced him to leave the field. In the days before substitutes, he returned ten minutes later, but now as a left-winger who was more a spectator than an active participant. Hardly able to move, Gillick was reduced to being more of a pest to opposing attacks than the creative force Rangers fans loved.

Despite this significant handicap, Rangers were still too good. Goals by Alex Venters, Willie Waddell and Jimmy Duncanson earned a 3-1 win and it was now just the Summer Cup left to complete the full set. Gillick was fit again in time for the closing stages of the tournament and he again showed his importance to the side.

In his return to the team in the quarter-final second leg, he scored twice in a 3-0 win over Falkirk at Ibrox. He then scored twice more before half-time in a 3-2 win over Albion Rovers in the Hampden semi-final, a match that saw future Ibrox team-mate Willie Findlay score for the Coatbridge men. That set up a repeat of the previous year's final, a showdown with a Hibs team that had finished the league season in second place and had, of course, handed Rangers that incredible 8-1 thrashing. This match would be a much closer affair, Gillick's fierce shot that grazed the post being the closest anyone came to scoring in 120 minutes of football in front of 60,000 at Hampden. The rules at the time stated that, in the event of a draw, the team who won more corners would be declared the victors. But both teams had won three corners apiece over the course of the match, which meant the trophy would be decided by the toss of a coin. Rangers captain Jock Shaw guessed correctly and the clean sweep was won.

Gillick was now as happy on and off the pitch as he had ever been, with a growing family at home and sensational form on the football field. He, like most Scottish football pundits, expected more glory in the 1942/43 season. They were absolutely right. All clubs saw their player pools depleted and, with some experienced players away in the services, youngsters with limited experience were often introduced to first-team duties. Rangers were no different, although most of the time they managed to field a relatively stable side, with many players having reserved occupations.

Gillick started the new campaign in blistering style, collecting another Glasgow Cup badge after scoring in convincing wins over Partick Thistle and Third Lanark in the semi-final and final, respectively. A 5-2 win over the Cathkin men sounds straightforward, but it took a Gillick goal four minutes from full time to finally see off a spirited Thirds comeback after they had scored twice to pull back an early Rangers three-goal lead. A last-minute Charlie Johnston strike added further icing on top of the celebration cake. Rangers were without Jerry Dawson and Willie Waddell that day; both were representing Scotland at Wembley in a 0-0 draw.

Torry's Glasgow Cup goals were nothing compared to the purple patch that followed. In late October, he scored four times in a single match for the first time in his Rangers career in a 7-0 demolition of Morton, then followed it up with a hat-trick in the next match against Hamilton. There was also a double against St Mirren and a fine finish in a win over Partick Thistle, meaning Gillick had crashed home ten goals in just five weeks.

And it wasn't just his goals that helped propel Rangers back to the top of the league again as 1942 drew to a close; Gillick's ability to find space and spot a killer pass was a massive factor in so many of the other goals the team scored. He picked up an injury in the St Mirren win in late November, not returning to the side until a huge Boxing Day clash at Easter Road between the top two in the table. The heavily outnumbered away fans in Edinburgh got to see what they had been missing in previous weeks when Gillick brilliantly set up Alex Venters to open the scoring. The match, sadly, was marred by crowd disorder in the second half, with Rangers goalkeeper Jerry Dawson knocked unconscious by a missile thrown from the crowd when Hibs had a goal that would have put them 2-1 ahead disallowed. Gillick and his colleagues were of a mind to walk off the pitch, but they were persuaded by the match officials that this would prompt even uglier scenes, so the match was played out as a draw, with neither side trying too hard to score.

As the year was now drawing to a close, it traditionally meant a clash of the Glasgow giants would herald the start of 1943. This New Year derby would be one that all in Rangers blue would long remember, especially Torry Gillick.

The match would, without doubt, become one of the highlights of Gillick's career, as Rangers achieved a record competitive score in the history of the fixture. Due to conditions imposed by the football authorities, the attendance was restricted, meaning just 30,000 were inside Ibrox to witness an historic day. If any of those spectators had enjoyed too much festive cheer and arrived at the stadium slightly late, they would have missed a blistering start by the home team. Rangers streaked into a two-goal lead inside the opening four minutes with goals from Duncanson and Waddell. Celtic rallied, however, and pulled a goal back in the 11th minute through left-winger David Duncan.

Rangers quickly regained control and dominated the remainder of the opening period. They came close several times to increasing their lead, but stout defending by the Celtic rearguard kept them at bay until the half-time whistle sounded. The crowd awaited the second half, wondering if Rangers would regret not turning their superiority into goals. The feeling inside the ground was that the next goal would prove crucial. No one, though, could have foreseen what would unfold over the next 45 minutes.

That crucial next goal arrived soon after the resumption; Gillick scored it but injured himself in the process by striking his head on an upright. He refused to leave the field and, as things turned out, he remained to make quite a mark on proceedings. A further 11 minutes had elapsed when George Young swept a free kick from fully 40 yards into the Celtic goalmouth. The ball may have taken the merest deflection off Waddell before it nestled in the net behind goalkeeper Willie Miller. It was 4-1 and things immediately got even worse for Celtic. Defender Malcolm McDonald must have presumably thought Waddell was standing offside, his protestations being so vociferous that he was eventually dismissed. Reports vary on whether the goal was scored by Young or Waddell, but the majority of articles give the goal to the big defender, which suggests that there was no deflection off Waddell at all.

Three minutes later, the visitors wing-half Matthew Lynch met the same disciplinary fate as his team-mate, again for remarks to the referee after the award of a free kick against him. Interestingly, there were reports following the match that Rangers forward Jimmy Duncanson felt the second dismissal was rather harsh and he had sent a letter to the SFA pleading for leniency on Lynch's behalf. He might have sought leniency from the authorities, but Duncanson and his team-mates showed no mercy on the pitch.

While the gulf in class was obvious prior to the dismissals, with Celtic now down to nine men it became a yawning chasm. Rangers were in no mood to take it easy and a great Waddell run ended with the winger crashing the ball past goalkeeper Miller, this one most definitely his goal. The 5-1 scoreline didn't last long, as shortly afterwards George Young converted a penalty for his second goal of the contest to make it 6-1.

The Rangers fans in the crowd were in full voice and, to a man, they rose to acclaim the injured Gillick who, despite being dazed, added a further two goals to complete his personal treble. One report of the match described Torry as 'operating … as if by instinct'. In modern football, this would likely be regarded as concussion and the player would be substituted. In 1943, the player stayed on and completed a hat-trick!

That day, Torry joined an elite band of Rangers players – one of only ten to achieve a competitive Old Firm match hat-trick. At the time of writing, Ally McCoist's Glasgow Cup Final treble was the last, in May 1986. This was his second hat-trick in the fixture, a feat matched only by the legendary RC Hamilton, who also notched two hat-tricks against Celtic. The other players who grabbed a personal treble on a single occasion were John Barker, Jimmy Duncanson, Johnny Hubbard, Willie Reid, Jimmy Fleming, Willie McIntosh and Willie Johnston.

Torry was to taste the other side of an eight-goal battering later that year in a different shade of blue when, along with Ibrox colleagues Adam Little, Willie Waddell and George Young, he was part of a Scotland team routed 8-0 by England at Maine Road in October. Dr Little reflected many years later: 'That afternoon at Maine Road, on paper we had a great Scots team. Tommy Walker and Torry Gillick were great international inside-forwards for Scotland. Willie Waddell was a powerful right-winger. George Young and Jimmy Carabine were great players. It was simply that Stan Cullis's England team was among the all-time greats.'

The 'Ne'erday' hammering of Celtic set Rangers firmly on course to again retain their Southern League crown, which was won by a comfortable five-point margin from Morton, the challenge from Hibs fading after that shameful Boxing Day clash. Torry's 20 league goals in just 21 appearances were a big reason why the trophy was to spend another year at Ibrox. In the Southern League Cup, Rangers and Celtic were drawn together in the initial group stages, meaning two more Old Firm derbies. The gulf in class between the teams remained evident. At Ibrox, a Gillick double helped ease Rangers to a comfortable 3-0 win at Ibrox, then it was an Alex Venters double that separated the sides in a 2-0 win in the return match at Parkhead. When Gillick scored the only goal in a 1-0 win over Hibs, it meant Rangers had won the group with maximum points.

Torry also grabbed a double in the semi-final win over Hamilton, although even the supremely talented and self-confident Gillick seemed slightly embarrassed when his opener found the net after it took a freak deflection off the boot of a Hamilton defender and looped over the helpless goalkeeper into the net. The closing stages could have proved tricky after Gillick's team-mate Adam Little was stretchered off, but a George Young penalty and a crisp Gillick last-minute finish saw Rangers through comfortably despite the man disadvantage.

This set up a Hampden final on Saturday, 8 May against Falkirk, with Rangers going for three wins out of three in the competition. In front of a smaller than expected attendance of just 18,000, Rangers took advantage of a strong wind in their favour in the first half to lay siege to the Falkirk goal. The only surprise at half-time was that they had only managed to breach the brave resistance of the Bairns once and it was a smartly taken Gillick goal that separated the teams. With the wind at their backs in the second half, Falkirk finally showed their attacking side and they scored an equaliser through Bobby Campbell. The remainder of the match saw both teams have chances but, after 90 minutes, it was Rangers who were declared winners by virtue of having won 11 corners compared to their opponents' three.

The first three trophies had been secured again, but there would be no clean sweep this time. The Charity Cup was won by Celtic for a rare Parkhead trophy win after Clyde stunned Ibrox with a 2-1 win in the first round. Gillick's temporary woes were increased when he suffered a rare Hampden disappointment in the Summer Cup Final; this time it was St Mirren's turn to upset the odds with a shock 1-0 win at the start of July. Torry missed most of the final competition of the season through injury, his only goal in the tournament being a winner at Tynecastle in the first round on the same day his old Everton team-mate Tommy Lawton guested for Morton and scored five times against Clyde.

Despite these two setbacks, Rangers were by far the dominant force in the land, with their players seemingly piling up massive medal collections. But this wasn't always the case. Speaking in 1972, the Ibrox outside-left in many of these wartime victories, Charlie Johnston, gave an interview. He recalled that players often got savings certificates instead of medals due to the scarcity of metals from which medals were made. On that basis, the Rangers playing staff must have been well on their way to becoming wealthy men.

The 1943/44 season came at a time when the tide was starting to turn in the war and there was the start of some optimism that the evil of Hitler might just be defeated. In the world of Scottish football, however, Rangers in the league championship still looked unbeatable. The season started in the usual way – a decisive win and Gillick goals. He scored in each of the opening three matches, the highlight being an opening-day double in a hugely impressive 4-0 win against Hibs, with another brace by Jimmy Duncanson completing their biggest win over the men from Easter Road since wartime competition started. The Glasgow Cup was again retained, Gillick scoring in the semi-final win over Partick Thistle with a thunderbolt shot from outside the penalty box. This set up a final showdown with Clyde, with the trophy secured thanks to a double by wartime striker Willie McIntosh, a player who had an impressive goals ratio during his spell in Royal Blue. The *Glasgow Herald* report of the 2-0 win described the play of Gillick and Waddell as 'brilliant'; not for the first or last time.

Rangers were comfortably at the top of the table when New Year arrived and, on a long winning run, when they travelled to Parkhead to face a Celtic team who must have been looking for revenge for the humiliation they had suffered a year earlier. The home fans in the 50,000 crowd were to again be disappointed and would again curse that man Gillick. After his hat-trick the previous New Year, the wily Rangers inside-right scored a crucial equaliser after Celtic had taken a surprise 1-0 lead. It was a pivotal moment, as Rangers then took control and raced away to a comfortable 3-1 success with second-half goals by Duncanson and young left-winger Murdoch McCormack. The title would be sewn up weeks before the last league fixture and, although Gillick's goal return of 11 in the championship was fewer than previous seasons, he was still a key player in Struth's all-conquering team.

Rangers opted not to play in the Summer Cup – the competition had seen falling attendances and dwindling interest – so there were only two more pieces of silverware on offer. The Southern League Cup certainly kept attracting the crowds and, after Gillick played his part in ensuring Rangers again topped their qualifying group, he lined up in the semi-final at Hampden against Celtic in an encounter that saw the football authorities limit the crowd to 90,000, as well as declaring that any 'flags or provocative emblems' would be removed from spectators before they could enter. The official attendance was given as just over 87,000, with no reported problems on the terraces. On the pitch, Gillick enjoyed yet another win over their city rivals, with a George Young penalty miss not enough to derail the unstoppable blue tide. Veteran centre-forward Jimmy Smith was back in the team and chipped in with two goals in a 4-2 victory in which the right-wing tandem of Waddell and Gillick caused their usual havoc to the beleaguered Celtic defence.

The Southern League Cup would then be relinquished for the first time when, after three successive wins, Gillick played in a tight and competitive final against Hibs at Hampden in front of 63,000 paying customers. The match ended 0-0, with Hibs scraping the victory by forcing one more corner than Rangers over the course of the match. That, perhaps, was no great surprise, given the fact that Rangers goalkeeper Jerry Dawson was carried off with a broken leg before 20 minutes had been played. The Ibrox men battled on with ten players and half-back Scot Symon in goal, but the numerical disadvantage proved just too much despite the best efforts of Gillick and his eight exhausted outfield team-mates.

The Charity Cup was regained, however, Gillick earning another honour in a final that saw the ever reliable Jimmy Smith score both goals in a close contest with Clyde that could have gone either way. This was obviously achieved without his friend and international team-mate Jerry Dawson, whose leg break meant he would miss many months of football. His long-time deputy George Jenkins would be the main custodian in the 1944/45 season.

Smith was more than just a goal machine at centre-forward; he was also a man who shared Torry's wicked sense of humour and ability to playfully mock the others who shared the Rangers dressing room. They made something of a comedy double act, often selecting a victim beforehand, then making him the target of their razor-sharp wit. Gillick was heard saying to him one day, 'Hey Smithie, you and me are at the wrong game. We could have made a fortune together on the stage. Me as the manager promoting you. We could have filled the Empire Theatre!'

It almost goes without saying that Rangers would go on to win the Southern League again that season. Similarly, it was inevitable that Gillick would start the season again with a goal, just as he had done in all but one wartime season at the club. The opening-day victims this time were Falkirk, Torry's goal an important counter as the match ended 3-2. He remained in decent form in the opening weeks, grabbing a double against St Mirren, as well as hitting the opener in a hard-fought 2-1 Glasgow Cup semi-final win against Partick. That set up a first final of the new campaign, with Celtic the opponents.

Torry had enjoyed an easy 4-0 win over them a few weeks earlier at Parkhead in the league, so he must have been confident of another Glasgow Cup triumph when the teams met at Hampden on 7 October 1944. That confidence seemed misplaced when Celtic roared into a 2-0 lead with just half an hour left to play. Torry had the relatively untried and unknown Neil McKinnon on the right wing outside him, with his usual wing partner Willie Waddell playing in an unaccustomed centre-forward role due to injuries and unavailability. This strange set-up took an hour to click into place; then, with all seemingly lost, the patchwork forward line caught fire. And, as was so often the case, it was a piece of Gillick magic that sparked it all off.

Just as the Rangers heads had started to go down, a sublime defence-splitting Gillick pass released Waddell, who ran clear of the Celtic defence, rounded goalkeeper Miller and crashed home a wonder goal from an impossible angle. The Rangers fans in the 60,000 Hampden crowd suddenly believed again and, in a devastating final push, their team rewarded that faith. Scot Symon equalised and then, with just a few minutes remaining, the relentless pressure on the Celtic defence saw them concede a penalty. Up stepped George Young and he made no mistake to cap off an incredible fightback and ensure more silverware for the Ibrox juggernaut.

The winning margin in the league this time was seven points, with the championship wrapped up in February when Dumbarton were blasted 6-3 at Boghead, a match that saw a Gillick double and a Duncanson treble. This early triumph meant that the title had been wrapped up in blue ribbons before the Southern League Cup campaign had started. After finally losing hold of the trophy the previous year to Hibs by the narrowest of margins, Gillick and his team-mates exacted revenge on the men from Easter Road by eliminating them in the group stage. The key result had been a 2-0 win at Ibrox where Gillick ran the show and Jimmy Smith hit both goals. After a straightforward win over Queen's Park in the last four, Motherwell awaited in the final on 12 May 1945.

The match was played just four days after the German surrender had signalled the end of almost six years of war in Europe, with the streets filled with happy and relieved partygoers celebrating the fall of Hitler. More than 70,000 turned up at Hampden on the Saturday to see the final, with a mood of celebration in the crowd. Rangers started the match as if they had enjoyed the festivities a little too much and deservedly went behind after 25 minutes. However, Motherwell failed to build on their advantage and were punished not long before the interval when Gillick ghosted into space in the penalty box to steer a perfect header into the net for the equaliser.

Most observers would have said at the end of the match that Motherwell deserved the trophy. But, despite forcing more corners and creating more chances, they failed to beat Jenkins in the Rangers goal in the second half. Rangers forward Alex Venters showed them how it was done when smashing home a rebound after a free kick was blocked, and the cup was heading back to Ibrox again.

The Gillick trophy haul for the season was completed in the Charity Cup later that month, Rangers completing another clean sweep of the tournaments they had entered. The victory was all the sweeter, as it came at the expense of great rivals Celtic. In a tight affair, the greater guile and craft of the Rangers forwards made the difference, with Gillick heavily involved in Jimmy Duncanson's opener before Alex Venters made the game safe. A late Celtic consolation made no difference to the wide smiles worn by Gillick and his team-mates at the final whistle.

The war had ended in Europe, but the conflict with Japan continued into August, with season 1945/46 being the last played under wartime regulations. The war did not formally come to an end until September 1945, with US General Douglas MacArthur accepting Japan's formal surrender aboard the US battleship *Missouri* anchored in Tokyo Bay. The general public could finally look forward to their longed-for return to normal life – and that included those yearning for a return of the national football competitions.

It would, of course, take some time to demob all the national servicemen but, with the war over, the man on the street could look forward to going along to a match without fears of an air raid or wondering how relatives were faring on the battlefield. With 25 September 1945 declared Victory Day, a series of exhibition games were arranged across the country to celebrate the event. On that date, Newcastle United came to Ibrox to take on Rangers.

The Geordies were one of England's top teams and the day before arriving in Glasgow they had annihilated Stoke City 9-1, so there were absolutely no doubts this would prove to be a tough match. A crowd of around 50,000 turned up and all admission money was donated to the King George VI Navy Fund, a worthy charity which benefitted immensely from the large crowd. Torry, of course, was part of the Rangers team faced with the challenge of defeating this formidable opponent.

Newcastle, though, were less than courteous visitors in the opening stages when they showed they were interested in just one thing, beating the mighty Rangers. After five minutes, legendary Magpies forward Jackie Milburn took a pass from Albert Stubbins and sent in a fierce left-foot shot from 20 yards which left Dawson helpless as the ball nestled in the net.

The gauntlet had well and truly been laid down and Rangers did not take long to respond. Just four minutes later, Scot Symon sent a superb pass through the middle and Billy Williamson raced on to it to send a powerful shot goalwards. Tom Swinburne got a hand to the shot but could not stop it crossing the line. It was already 1-1 and the game was well and truly on.

The match was everything the press had promised it would be, both sides attacking each other for all they were worth. Dawson was forced to make a fine save from Milburn just before Ibrox winger Chris McNee had a shot deflected narrowly wide.

In the 23rd minute, Rangers took the lead. Great work by Jimmy Duncanson left three Newcastle defenders in his wake and his cutback across the face of goal left Billy Williamson with the easiest of chances. Rangers now had the upper hand and the visitors had no answer to the right-wing duo of Waddell and Gillick, who were taking the Magpies' defence apart. After the half-time break, the light blues continued to press forward and, in the 50th minute, only the woodwork denied Williamson a hat-trick.

Three minutes later, Waddell raced into the penalty area and was impeded by full-back Smith. There was to be no celebration, though, as Young's spot-kick was saved by Swinburne. This seemed to galvanise Newcastle and they clawed their way back into the game. A lapse in the Rangers defence allowed inside-forward Charlie Weyman space to shoot and his effort flew into Dawson's net to tie the scores. Disappointed though the crowd were, they couldn't help but appreciate the quality of football on show and Rangers were not prepared to settle for a share of the spoils.

Towards the end, the light blues forced a corner and Willie Waddell's cross into the box was met by the high-flying Jimmy Duncanson, whose thumping header restored the Ibrox side's lead. The roar which greeted the goal was said to almost split the skies and this time Newcastle could not come back. Rangers ran out worthy winners.

The match gave the Glasgow public a glimpse of what normality would look like and they were hugely appreciative of what both sides had served up. The Scottish and English press were united in acclaiming Rangers for beating one of England's top sides and, although he didn't score, Gillick was named in virtually all reports as one of the game's best players, with the *Glasgow Herald* stating that the partnership of Waddell and Gillick had 'run wild'.

In the spirit of introducing more glamour matches for the masses to enjoy before domestic seasons could properly return, next up were the famous Russian side Moscow Dynamo at Ibrox on 28 November 1945. To this day, the match is still regarded as one of the most famous club friendly matches ever played in Scotland.

Dynamo arrived in Glasgow to a warm welcome, including a city chambers reception, but a major row broke out on the eve of the match when the Soviets refused to allow winger Jimmy Caskie to play. Everton had just confirmed the sale of Caskie and Gillick on permanent transfers to Rangers but, while Torry had been playing in the Ibrox first team for many years during the war, Caskie had played for both St Mirren and Hibs as a guest, turning out for the Easter Road team just four weeks earlier, and had yet to play a competitive match for Rangers.

They insisted Caskie was still a guest player, something that they felt strongly about after facing an Arsenal team with five guests, including Stanley Matthews and Stan Mortensen, a few days earlier in London. Although the Russians still won that game 4-3, they felt they had been tricked by the strength of the opposition and harboured a sense of mistreatment. Guest players would not be permitted or Dynamo would not play. No amount of diplomacy could budge the Russians and, facing the threat of a game for which 95,000 tickets had already been sold being cancelled, Rangers had to accept that Caskie would miss the match. In fairness, although the press had reported that Everton had agreed the double sale of Gillick and Caskie a few days earlier, the Goodison board's minutes stated that the cheque for £5,000 had not been received until 18 December, which would suggest that Caskie would indeed have been a guest player when the Russians were in Glasgow. So would Gillick, but his five years in the Rangers first team made him far more a Ranger than a guest by this time.

The visitors made a great impression on their Scottish hosts with their meticulous attention to detail, even bringing their own food with them. Observers at their training sessions had noted their athletic prowess and skilful technique and many wondered how the

Rangers players would cope, as they had remained part-time after the war ended.

As it was a midweek match, thousands took time off work – officially or unofficially – and shops factories, offices and shipyards were deserted. The atmosphere inside a packed stadium was electric. Dynamo astonished the 95,000 spectators by carrying out an extensive warm-up prior to kick-off that lasted over 15 minutes, something that was rarely seen in football at the time.

This helped the visitors make a whirlwind start when the match got under way and they took the lead after just two minutes. Jerry Dawson may have wished he had also warmed up, as a free kick by Vasili Kartsev caught him cold, the goalkeeper looking badly at fault as the ball hit the Rangers net. Ibrox was stunned into a brief silence, but soon Rangers were the ones on the attack. In unfamiliar blue and white hoops, the Ibrox men roared back and were awarded a penalty just five minutes later for a foul on Bobby Williamson. The kick was entrusted to Willie Waddell, who was left shaking his head when the famous Russian custodian Alexei 'Tiger' Khomich pulled off a miraculous save by tipping the winger's shot on to the crossbar.

The contest was now in full flow, with the massive crowd in full voice to match. Rangers mounted quick and direct attacks, whereas the Russians employed a more methodical and scientific style of play. After 24 minutes, the crowd were stunned by a swift and skilful counter-attacking move involving all five of the Moscow forwards which ended in Kartsev applying a clinical finish from 15 yards. Rangers were 2-0 down and the unbeatable reputation of the Russians looked to be justified.

But William Struth's men were not going to crumble; they simply rolled up their sleeves and refused to contemplate defeat. They were rewarded five minutes before the interval when that prolific veteran centre-forward Jimmy Smith bundled the ball into the net after an accurate long through pass from skipper Jock Shaw. At half-time, many felt that the next goal would be crucial and that there were signs the Russians were starting to lose their confidence in the face of this unrelenting Rangers comeback.

Those signs grew stronger in the second period, Dynamo appearing to wilt as Rangers gained more and more control of the game, with wingers Waddell and Johnston now creating havoc. Khomich was outstanding and his full-blooded tussles with Smith would live long in the memory of those fortunate to be inside Ibrox. Substitutes had been agreed upon before the match and this created a famous moment of controversy in the 51st minute.

Torry Gillick was seen in the centre circle visibly counting the Russian players with his right arm and finger raised. He then attracted the attention of the referee, Tommy Thompson, and started an animated conversation with the official that soon also involved a linesman. Speaking in 1967, Torry explained when asked how, in the frantic pace of the game, he managed to spot the Russian 'error' of having an extra player in their team: 'I began to feel my style was being cramped. There did not seem to be the same space

– and I can count up to 12!' He was absolutely right; there had been a substitution made without anyone leaving the park. Only the Dynamo players and officials could know for sure whether this was intentional, but most Scots suspected it was a desperate tactic to combat the Rangers onslaught. It was 11 versus 11 again once the referee agreed with Torry's arithmetic and removed one sheepish Russian from the field.

With the numbers level again, Rangers continued to dominate but struggled to find the equaliser they deserved. It finally arrived with 15 minutes left when referee Thomson awarded the home team a second penalty. The Dynamo players argued furiously over the award but George Young was unaffected by the delay and slammed the ball past Khomich to tie the match at 2-2 and ensure honours were even after a classic and legendary occasion.

In April 1946, Torry got the chance to meet his old Everton team-mates again when Rangers travelled to Belfast for a testimonial match to honour Irish League secretary Jack Price. The match at Windsor Park saw Rangers and Everton play out an entertaining match, with Gillick's display described by a reporter from the *Evening Express* as 'perfection'. He may have been at his imperious best, but he was on the wrong end of a 3-2 defeat, with one of Everton's goals scored from the penalty spot by his great friend Gordon Watson. It wasn't often Gordon got more of the limelight than his lifelong friend and he let Torry know afterwards how good it felt!

Although these friendlies provided glamour, there was a domestic season being played, one that Rangers wanted to dominate again. Despite Torry enjoying a first-round victory over Celtic in the Glasgow Cup, then scoring in the semi-final against Clyde, Rangers lost their grip on the trophy when the Shawfield men prevailed 4-3 in a thrilling match. Gillick hit 15 goals in the league campaign as Rangers completed the full set of seven wartime championships by easing to a comfortable eight-point winning margin over Hibs.

The foundation for the title success was built on an impressive unbeaten run from the start of September through to early January, with Gillick's goals featuring prominently during this purple patch. He hit the opposition net nine times in the nine league matches played before Christmas, with 5-1 wins against Hamilton, Partick Thistle and Kilmarnock all including a Gillick double. The Kilmarnock match on Saturday, 15 December was a particularly happy occasion for the Ibrox faithful; not only did they witness another easy victory, but they were able to welcome back Willie Thornton to the forward line after his heroic wartime exploits on foreign fields. It was his first game in a Rangers shirt since January 1943.

Going into the New Year, Celtic were the only distant challenger and most observers agreed that a Rangers win in the first match of 1946 would effectively settled the title race. The 75,000 Parkhead crowd saw a relatively tame affair compared to many of the recent battles between the pair, but they also saw a familiar outcome. After

27 minutes, two truly great Rangers players combined to score the game's only goal. Gillick and Thornton moved down the Celtic left with clever interplay before Thornton chipped a delightful pass inside the Celtic full-back for Torry to bear down on goal. His low shot was brilliantly blocked by a last-gasp tackle by Jimmy Mallan but the ball ran to the onrushing Thornton, who cleverly dispatched it past goalkeeper Miller. The war hero became the New Year scoring hero as the Rangers fans celebrated another Old Firm success. Gillick was given rave reviews for his display, with one report describing him as 'outstanding' and remarking that 'Celtic had nothing to compare'.

Gillick also continued his fine form in the Southern League Cup competition, both in goals and match-winning displays. His four goals in the tournament included a vital strike to help conquer Dundee in the last eight before firing an extra-time winner against Hearts in the semi-final at Hampden before 75,000 fans. It was a match where his display was described in one Monday report as being 'brilliant in his manipulation of the ball'. Unfortunately, he picked up an injury before the end and missed the final in which Aberdeen surprised the enormous 135,000 crowd by snatching a 3-2 triumph with a late winner. His absence was undoubtedly a factor in the cup heading north.

The Charity Cup was retained, however, Gillick returning in time to enjoy a final victory over Third Lanark. The last wartime competition was now under way, with the Victory Cup competition organised to celebrate the end of wartime football restrictions. With precious metals in rare supply, however, the SFA were unable to organise a trophy for this tournament, so the decision was made to use the same cup that had been used for the Southern League Cup competition. This was much to Aberdeen's frustration, as they had assumed that, by winning the recent final against Rangers, they would get to keep the trophy forever.

The competition had started prior to the Charity Cup Final, Gillick missing the first two rounds while recovering from his injury. He missed the second-round tie at Airdrie, which was a straightforward win but a momentous occasion for three wonderful Rangers players. Jimmy Smith, the man with the best goals-to-games ratio of all the club's legendary goalscorers, played his last first-team game. He scored, of course. Meanwhile, goalkeeper Bobby Brown and defender Sammy Cox made their debuts, both men going on to become key components in the legendary Iron Curtain defence of the post-war years.

Torry did return for the quarter-finals and he scored in both the initial draw and the replay win against Falkirk. That set up a semi-final against Celtic, which would turn out to be one of the most controversial of all the Old Firm occasions in Gillick's long career. The teams clashed at Hampden on Saturday, 1 June and the 90,000 fans saw a one-sided affair that became a contest between the Rangers forward line and the inspired Celtic goalkeeper Willie Miller. Gillick and his the rest of the Rangers forward line left the pitch frustrated that the custodian defied their every effort with several breathtaking stops. It ended 0-0 and a replay was required.

Around 50,000 travelled back to Hampden four nights later and few could have imagined the events that would unfold before their eyes. The first half was similar to the previous Saturday, with Rangers enjoying most of the play. This time they made their domination count when an inch-perfect Gillick pass split the Celtic defence wide open and put Waddell through with just Miller to beat. The Rangers and Scotland winger made no mistake with a clinical finish. By the interval, this was still the only goal, Torry being unlucky to see a shot rattle the crossbar with Miller well beaten. But Celtic were now toiling badly, not only being outplayed but hampered by an injury to forward Jackie Gallagher which left him limping badly.

Gallagher bravely tried to soldier on in the second half, but he had to admit defeat and leave the pitch ten minutes after the restart. Ten minutes later, all hell broke loose. Referee Matthew Dale had somehow refused Rangers a penalty in the first half when Miller blatantly grabbed at Gillick's ankles as he attempted to round the goalkeeper. Now he decided to point to the spot when Willie Thornton fell to the ground under the challenge of two Celtic defenders. It looked quite a soft award and it prompted a furious reaction from the Celtic players. Captain George Paterson picked up the ball and refused to hand it over to the referee while arguing loudly about the decision. Paterson was sent off. Meanwhile, team-mate Jimmy Mallan was dragging his studs across the penalty spot trying to obliterate it and, when challenged by the beleaguered Mr Dale, he grabbed the ball and kicked it away. He was also sent off.

The remaining Celtic players looked briefly as if they were going to walk off the pitch, their behaviour now causing mayhem on the terraces. Thankfully, they saw sense and this allowed George Young to finally take the spot kick. He scored, despite the incredible pressure that must have been on him as police battled with rioting Celtic supporters behind one goal. The goal prompted a minor pitch invasion, with several Celtic fans arrested as the police slowly restored some semblance of order. One fan seemed to be heading for the referee with a bottle in his hand; mercifully, he was intercepted.

With Rangers two goals in front and now playing against eight men, their supporters must have thought this was the perfect opportunity to hand out another drubbing. But, perhaps wisely in the circumstances, the Rangers players decided not to exert themselves in the closing stages, content to keep the ball and to avoid anything that might spark more trouble. Mr Dale was obviously not too keen on any more time in the spotlight either, as he ignored a seemingly blatant Rangers penalty in the dying moments. Given the likely consequences of pointing to the spot, his turning a blind eye was understandable. The match ended 2-0, with Gillick and his colleagues likely relieved to get back to the dressing rooms unscathed.

Both the dismissed Celtic players would be given lengthy bans by the SFA in a subsequent disciplinary hearing, with the SFA also dismissing wild accusations that were being made about the referee being drunk!

When the carnage of the semi-final was over, Rangers had reached the final of the Victory Cup and the Hampden showpiece would see them up against Hibs ten days later. There were more than 100,000 inside the stadium for the last wartime final between opponents who would go on to dominate once the traditional competitions resumed.

The first half was an even affair, both sides enjoying spells of pressure. It was Rangers who grabbed the opener, however, when a Jimmy Caskie cross midway through the half was met by Gillick and his header beat the despairing dive of Jimmy Kerr. The lead was cancelled out before the interval, however, thanks to a fine strike by Johnny Aitkenhead. As the huge crowd cheered the teams from the field, many thought that whoever scored next would likely prevail. Within seconds of the restart, the next goal arrived.

Straight from kick-off, the ball was laid back to Scot Symon who aimed an accurate long pass to the edge of the Hibs penalty area, where it was won by the head of Willie Thornton. He nodded it back into the path of Jimmy Duncanson whose unstoppable shot flew high into the Hibs net from 20 yards. It was a goal fit to grace any cup final. No Hibs player had touched the ball since the teams had retaken the field after the break and they found themselves a goal behind again.

Hibs pushed forward as time ticked away, but it was Rangers who continued to look the more potent. Waddell had a goal disallowed for reasons not obvious to the spectators before he threaded a delightful pass through to Duncanson in the 86th minute that allowed the inside-forward to take control, round Kerr and slot it into the waiting goal. Victory was now assured and the 3-1 win meant the trophy would now be the permanent property of the club. Gillick was one of 11 players who picked up a unique prize in the history of the Scottish game, a Victory Cup winner's medal.

Rangers had dominated the wartime competitions, winning 25 out of 34 first-team competitions they entered. It is also worth noting that, during the Regional League era, Rangers were in the fortunate position that their reserve team continued to operate and competed against the first teams of northerly clubs such as Aberdeen, Dunfermline and Dundee in the North Eastern League. Remarkably, the Ibrox reserves won the title in 1941/42 and also lifted the Mitchell and Supplementary cups in 1943/44.

Such was the nature of the times folk were living in, sometimes the reserve team attendances would outstrip the first team. For example, on 6 December 1941, 5,000 watched the first team at Love Street while 10,000 attended Ibrox for the second team's match against Aberdeen.

This Rangers domination over Scottish football included a vast superiority over their great city rivals. The stranglehold over Celtic was best illustrated not just by the 8-1 win in 1943, but by the match on 7 May 1942. The reserves beat Celtic 2-0 in the Second Eleven

Cup despite Celtic fielding the only team they had due to their financial problems – their first team!

Torry was a massive part of that supremacy and, by the time the wartime competitions ended, he was the club's top scorer across the various temporary tournaments. His 86 goals in the Southern League and 26 in the Southern League Cup were more than any other Rangers player in either of the two main wartime competitions.

In March 1946, not long after he had signed back on as a permanent Rangers player, he was offered the chance to go to the other side of the world and play in Australia for Leichardt in the city of Sydney. But, despite the money on offer, Torry had little hesitation in turning them down; he was enjoying life far too much, both as a footballer at Ibrox and as a father, with his young family now settled in Glasgow. It was a decision he would never regret.

Years later, when reminiscing about the great wartime Rangers team, captain Jock Shaw said, 'During this spell, we simply dominated the game and we won everything going. There were some great names around then. There was Jerry Dawson in goal and Dougie Gray at right-back while at centre-half there was either Willie Woodburn or George Young … on the right wing there was Willie Waddell and, when he intermittently came back from the war, there was Willie Thornton at centre. Alex Venters was in the team when I arrived and then there was Torry Gillick. They were all terrific players.' He added, 'As well as everyone being a top-class player, we were a team as well. We all worked for each other and helped each other, too. And the players could take a telling. It didn't matter who they were or what their reputation was. If they did something wrong on the park, they were told in no uncertain manner. And they listened.'

Another stalwart of the wartime Rangers team was winger Charlie Johnston, who made his debut for the club in the match at Falkirk in 1940, which was Gillick's first game after his return. Speaking in the 1970s, Johnston said, 'Scottish football was littered with some of the greatest personality players in its history during that spell and nowhere were there more of these colourful characters on view than right here at the stadium.' He was then asked which Ibrox team-mate was the biggest character of all and his answer was unequivocal. 'That just had to be Torry Gillick. What a player Torry was. And he was a law unto himself. He seemed to get away with things that nobody else in the team could. Not that anybody minded, for Torry had so much talent that sometimes we just used to look at him in amazement after he had performed some trick or other. 'In many of the games we played, we would get 20 minutes of magic from Torry, then he would drop back and go and hide. The thing being, we would have scored one or maybe two during Torry's 20 minutes and that meant the game was won.' An individual star in a team packed with great players, who all had a willingness to put the team first, Gillick was a unique cog in a well-oiled winning machine. It was a recipe for success during those war years. And it would continue to be a winning recipe after the wartime restrictions finally ended.

CHAPTER 8
IN FRONT OF THE CURTAIN

ON SATURDAY, 10 August 1946, Scottish football finally emerged from the dark shadow of war when the new 16-team Scottish 'A' Division played the opening day fixtures. Rangers were favourites in the eyes of many, with the team looking to bring a league title back to Ibrox for a ninth successive season when the triumphs of the temporary wartime competitions were included. In a season's preview in the *Glasgow Herald*, the writer stated that Victory Cup runners-up Hibs and Southern League Cup winners Aberdeen were seen as the most realistic challengers to break the Rangers stranglehold, which would prove prophetic when the end-of-season league table was viewed. Those teams did, indeed, fill the first three places.

The opening day was much-anticipated, with a tricky visit to Fir Park seen as a decent early test for the men in blue. Gillick was in his customary inside-right position while several Rangers stars made their official debuts. One of these was goalkeeper Bobby Brown, a man who would become a great friend of Gillick's both during and after his remaining years at the club. Brown would not only go on to enjoy a stellar Ibrox playing career, he would become a huge success in management, including a spell in charge of the Scotland national team. Many years after his football career had ended, he gave an interview about his time in the game. When speaking about the many greats he shared a dressing room with, he made sure to mention Gillick.

'Inside-forward Torry Gillick was a real character,' said Brown, 'and he was also an extremely talented footballer but an equally lazy trainer! Despite that, over a distance of 30 yards he was like greased lightning.' The goalkeeper shared Torry's love of fishing, something that no doubt helped keep their friendship going well after they stopped playing together. When Brown had a spell as St Johnstone manager in the 1960s, the pair would often meet up to cast a line into the River Tay.

For the opener at Motherwell, around 30,000 crammed into the stadium and they watched a thrilling match lit up by some wonderful Rangers attacking play. One match report proclaimed the 'brilliant individual movements of Waddell, Gillick and Thornton'. The two Willies saw their excellence rewarded with a goal apiece and, with the addition of a double from the deadly Jimmy Duncanson, William Struth's men cruised to a 4-2 victory.

Reflecting the popularity of post-war football in Scotland, the following midweek saw more than 200,000 people flock to the eight top division matches, with 70,000 of them at Ibrox to see Hibs underline their title credentials with a 2-1 win, which came despite Gillick winning an early penalty for the home side which was converted by George Young. The wily inside-forward gave another performance of great skill and intelligence, with reports saying only the brilliance of Hibs goalkeeper Jimmy Kerr prevented Gillick being the best player on view.

The last official league goal of Gillick's Rangers career had come in his final appearance of his first spell at the club in December 1935 at Perth and, after almost 11 years, his name appeared again on a Scottish League scoresheet in the third match of the season when he hit the vital second goal in a home 3-2 win against Kilmarnock. With Hibs winning again to keep their 100 per cent record, it was becoming obvious already that Rangers were in a scrap for the championship.

After those three league matches, Gillick had the following Saturday off when the Glasgow Cup first round ties were played, with Rangers receiving a bye. It was maybe just as well the team had a free Saturday; Jock Shaw, Sammy Cox, Willie Waddell and Willie Thornton had been selected to play in an England v Scotland match at Maine Road to raise funds for those affected by the terrible disaster earlier in the year at a Bolton Wanderers match that had seen 33 fans crushed to death. It was the kind of horrific tragedy that future manager Waddell and assistant Thornton would live through on a more personal level at Ibrox in January 1971.

After that early loss to Hibs, Rangers had lost twice more by the end of September. Defeats at Pittodrie and Firhill, both in front of more than 35,000 fans, meant that Hibs, Aberdeen, Thistle and Rangers were all locked at the top on the same points total. Modern fans accustomed to an annual two-horse race for the Scottish title would struggle to recognise the far more competitive league of 1946. The Partick defeat, in a match rearranged from August, came despite Gillick and Duncanson both scoring fine goals in the first half. The pair were in excellent early-season form and had shared four goals the previous weekend in a rout of St Mirren. That result had seen Rangers go top for the first time.

Sandwiched in between these two defeats, Gillick played in the first peacetime Old Firm match for seven years and it must have been a surreal experience for him that afternoon at Parkhead. Firstly, the opposition went into the match having lost all three of their home matches in the league so far, leaving them near the foot of the league table. Secondly, the Rangers team were without two of their deadliest attacking weapons, centre-forward Willie Thornton and Gillick's right-wing partner Willie Waddell. It meant rare starts for a couple of fringe players, with Jimmy Parlane – father of 1970s idol Derek – chosen to lead the line and Angus Stead given his chance on the right wing. And, lastly, the attendance was a fraction of the crowd that would be expected, with just 30,000 paying customers. This was partly due to the match being boycotted by the Rangers FC Supporters Association after Celtic had looked to cash in on the attendance boom by significantly increasing admission prices.

This all made the occasion unusual, but there was nothing unusual about the result or the performance of the Rangers inside-right. A double by Jimmy Duncanson and a strike by deputy forward Parlane gave Rangers a 3-2 win, with Gillick effortlessly adapting to a new right-winger to the extent that the Monday match report stated Stead and Gillick 'struck a happy partnership'. It continued by saying 'their understanding led to the brightest combined football of the game'. By the time Rangers played their first match in the new Scottish League Cup competition in late September, they were top of the table as the cut-throat nature of the division saw surprise results almost every week. Gillick, of course, was one of the 11 men who made club history by starting that debut match in a tournament that is now firmly established as the first leg of the domestic treble. The initial format of the new cup competition saw group stages of four teams, with Rangers hosting St Mirren in the opener at Ibrox. Rangers eased to a comfortable 4-0 win, with defender Sammy Cox the unlikely scorer of the first goal in a tournament that Rangers would go on to dominate in years to come.

Gillick didn't score that night, but he then enjoyed a burst of goalscoring form, hitting the net seven times in eight games. These included his first-ever goal in the League Cup, hitting an early second-half equaliser at Hampden against Queen's Park before creating the first of Willie Thornton's late double that sealed a 4-2 win. He then followed that up with two more League Cup goals in an easy 4-0 win in Paisley as Rangers raced towards qualification to the quarter-finals. In the league, he scored one and was reported to be 'superb' as Hamilton were hit for six before a vital Gillick winner in a tight tussle at Dumfries allowed Rangers to retain their narrow lead at the top.

Going into the festive period, that lead had grown to three points and it was Gillick who would be the main man in royal blue over Christmas and New Year. First, there would be a titanic tussle with Hibs in mid-December, a match watched by a then-record Easter Road crowd of just under 42,000. In a match that justified that old description of 'a game of two halves', Rangers dominated the first period with the Waddell and Gillick pairing in unplayable form. One match report stated 'the Rangers right wing (do they have a left wing these days?) bewildered their opponents with their quick, short passing'. It was no surprise that the opening goal came from more right-wing Gillick and Waddell magic which saw Gillick delivering a devilish cross that Duncanson headed home with the aid of a deflection. That slender lead was welcome after the break, Gillick forced into a more defensive role as the home team battered the Iron Curtain until gaining a late equaliser.

In the four league fixtures that followed in late December and early January, Torry scored in all of them. A vital late winner against Falkirk at Ibrox and the only Rangers goal in a 1-1 draw away to Third Lanark meant Gillick was the last Rangers goalscorer of 1946. Then, as 1947 arrived with the traditional battle of the Glasgow giants, he was the man who mattered again in a fiercely competitive 'Ne'erday' clash at Ibrox.

The Ibrox crowd of 85,000 was the largest attendance for any club match in Britain so far that season, with the majority unhappy at the interval as underdogs Celtic held a 1-0 lead. Then, on the hour, a Jimmy Duncanson header fell into the path of Gillick and he thundered the ball into the Celtic net. The match ended 1-1 and, the next day, he scored two more at Rugby Park in a 2-0 win that saw Kilmarnock's all-time attendance record broken and many fans spilling from the terraces and standing near the touchline. One match report made the rather obvious statement that the two-goal hero had given 'another fine display'. With the hectic holiday fixtures completed, Rangers remained three points clear, their lead entirely down to the goals of their inside-right.

By the time March came around, the title was looking assured, but hopes of adding the Scottish Cup were dashed when Hibs won an Easter Road replay 2-0 in front of more than 50,000 fans packed liked sardines into the Edinburgh stadium. It was a match Gillick missed through injury, picking up a knock to his back in the midweek League Cup quarter-final success over Dundee United. He had been replaced for the Hibs match by Jimmy Parlane, with one match report stating quite simply: 'Rangers missed Gillick in the attack.' This result meant Hibs were unbeaten in four matches against Rangers that season and, when the teams were drawn together in the semi-final of the League Cup, it was a match the Scottish football public were desperate to see.

The Hampden attendance for this clash of the Scottish heavyweights saw an incredible 125,154 people fill the vast slopes of the national stadium. This would not only be the biggest crowd of the season; to this day it remains the biggest crowd ever to watch a Scottish League Cup match. Rangers were determined to finally get one over their rivals, with the newspaper articles in the lead-up to the match all focussing on whether Hibs had the measure of their Glasgow opponents.

The daily headlines and massive attendance might have been why the match started in such breakneck fashion. The referee was forced to stop play for several heavy tackles, with even Gillick caught up in the frenzy of it all when he committed a challenge on Sammy Kean which the *Glasgow Herald* described as an 'inexcusable foul'. But football did eventually break out and it was Gillick, showing the more recognisable side to his game, who broke the deadlock. After 19 minutes, he ghosted into the penalty area to get on the end of a Billy Williamson cross and head the ball past Jimmy Kerr. This set Rangers on their way and, by half-time, that other deadly duo Willie Thornton and Willie Waddell had added further goals to finish the match as a contest. Waddell limped off at half-time and was a virtual spectator during the second period, a pulled muscle meaning Rangers were effectively playing with ten men. But with skipper Jock Shaw at his tigerish best, Hibs could only manage a late consolation effort as the majority of the record crowd roared their approval at a convincing win.

It meant Gillick now had the opportunity to add a new medal to his collection; the first League Cup Final would be against Aberdeen just a fortnight later. It would be a bittersweet weekend for him, with the death of his father, Lawrence, on the day before the match. Determined to play, Gillick declared himself available for a game played in pouring rain and a driving wind, which undoubtedly affected the attendance. More than 30,000 ticket holders decided not to make the journey in such foul weather, meaning the final crowd of 82,684 was regarded as disappointing. As well as dealing with heartache off the field, Gillick had a challenge on the pitch, with young outside-right Eddie Rutherford his wing partner, as Waddell's semi-final injury had not yet healed.

Aberdeen captain Frank Dunlop won the toss and bizarrely decided to give Rangers the benefit of the gale force wind in the first half, presumably thinking this would give his side the advantage in the vital closing stages. The flaw in this plan was that it allowed Rangers to dominate the first half and the final was effectively over by the interval. With the wind in his face, Aberdeen goalkeeper George Johnstone struggled to get his goal kicks to land more than 30 yards from his goal and one such clearance midway through the first half ended in Gillick making history. Johnstone's clearance was held up in the wind and fell towards defender Joe McLaughlin. He failed to control the ball and was dispossessed by the ever-alert Willie Thornton. He played it wide to Jimmy Duncanson, whose cross found the inrushing Gillick's forehead and the first goal ever scored in a League Cup Final belonged to the Rangers inside-forward.

By the time Gillick and his team-mates left the pitch to seek the warmth of the dressing room, they had a commanding 3-0 lead. The second goal, scored by Billy Williamson, owed a lot to a typically accurate Gillick through pass to winger Rutherford. That reliable goalscorer on the big occasion, Jimmy Duncanson, added a third. Duncanson scored again in the second half as Rangers cruised to the first national honour of the post-war football era. Gillick had again shown his importance to a team who were accustomed to lifting trophies, with his shrewd use of the ball in desperately difficult conditions highlighted in several match reports. One praised the way he 'nursed his young winger cleverly' and of how in the second half, when the conditions forced the team to defend, Gillick had 'played a semi half-back game'.

One trophy became two as the league title was soon also confirmed, Gillick playing 27 of the 30 league matches and scoring an impressive and important 17 times. With the championship won by just two points from Hibs, it marked the end of another year of winners' medals for Gillick and his team-mates; it also marked the beginning of a great Glasgow-Edinburgh rivalry that dominated the Scottish game for several years. Gillick playing in front of the best defence in the country, up against an Easter Road team built around a forward line who would go on to earn the 'Famous Five' nickname.

There was still one more trophy up for grabs, with the end-of-season Charity Cup providing an Old Firm final in mid-May. On a pitch that had been battered by rain all day, Gillick produced the moment of magic that decided the tie in front of 40,000 shivering souls. He took a Duncanson pass, feinted to go one way before going the other and unleashing a venomous shot that goalkeeper Willie Miller brilliantly kept out. The Celtic stopper had no luck, however, as the rebound fell to Gillick's ex-Everton colleague Jimmy Caskie, who slotted it into the gaping goal for the only score of the 90 minutes.

With Gillick now into his 30s, he was the 'old man' of the forward line, his wise head in perfect harness with the running power of Waddell, Thornton, Duncanson and Caskie. As he got older, Torry relied more and more on his vision and reading of the game to ensure he was in the perfect space to receive the ball and to play the killer pass. He also found himself upstairs at Ibrox in the manager's office at regular intervals, Struth's authoritarian style often clashing with the player's attitude towards his rules. It was never a relationship that harboured any resentment or ill feelings; the two men seemed to take some enjoyment out of their battles.

One rule that Gillick particularly disliked was the strict dress code expected of all Rangers players, a code that included the wearing of a bowler hat on the way to and from the stadium. He found himself in hot water on several occasions, the wily old manager having the perfect view along Copland Road from his office, from where he would spy on arriving players. Anyone not appropriately dressed could expect his wrath, and usually a fine, with Gillick so out of pocket with his frequent punishments that he eventually had to come up with a way to fool the boss. He would leave the house in his favoured flat cap, the bowler hat in a paper bag. When nearing Copland Road, he would then swap hats, the cap going in the bag and the bowler on to his head, just as he came into view from the stadium.

One other aspect of daily life at the club also proved to be an area of disagreement between manager and player. Gillick was never the most committed and hardworking in training; he enjoyed a ball at his feet but not the regular fitness work of running that the club trainer insisted upon. He perfected the art of being late out of the dressing room and joining the laps of the track after the others had already circled the pitch a few times, although when caught out he would often find himself running alone to make up for the laps he had missed.

Torry also fell victim to the kidology of Struth on one occasion when he declared himself unfit prior to a match. Hobbling into the dressing room, he told trainer Jimmy Smith he was 'crippled' and would be unable to take part. He was immediately told to report upstairs to Struth. The bold Torry stated he 'couldnae crawl up the stairs, far less walk up them'. Smith was adamant that he should see the boss. A few minutes later, Torry returned downstairs to announce: 'That old so and so would have you playing unless your bones were sticking out of your stockings.' That may or may not have been a fair accusation, but Gillick played on the Saturday and scored the winning goal!

The other main reason he and Struth clashed was over money. The club had a strict policy around player wages, with basic pay supplemented by appearance money and win bonuses. These extra payments obviously stopped during the close season, when players went back to basic wage only. Gillick discovered that some players were getting paid more than others during the summer and, when he challenged Struth, he was told that the most senior players in the team deserved a little extra. Gillick's response was to point out these players weren't more important when there was no football being played!

The 1946/47 season had been a triumph for the club, and for Gillick, and his influence was still very much to the fore in 1947/48. This would be a season where he would create another record and it would start in familiar fashion, with another Ibrox win over Celtic. The teams were drawn in the same group of the League Cup competition, the crowd of almost 80,000 being a British record attendance for an opening-day match. Gillick wasn't on the scoresheet in a 2-0 victory; in fact, his main mention in the match reports was for earning a stern lecture from the referee for questioning one of his decisions too loudly. Both goals were scored by another big-match specialist, centre-forward Billy Williamson.

The initial weeks of the season were interrupted for Gillick by injury, meaning he missed the first Old Firm league encounter, which was again won 2-0. Williamson was on the scoresheet again that day, but it was an occasion remembered best for what happened at the other end of the pitch. This was the first competitive match that saw the famous 'Iron Curtain' defence take to the field. All six players had been at the club the previous season, but various circumstances and the excellent contributions at half-back from Scot Symon and Willie Rae had combined to prevent this combination from being seen. Goalkeeper Bobby Brown, full-backs George Young and Jock Shaw, with a half-back line of Ian McColl, Willie Woodburn and Sammy Cox kept a clean sheet in the Old Firm match. They would go on to frustrate opposing attacks for some time.

The Iron Curtain nickname was copied from a phrase used by Winston Churchill in a speech he made in Fulton, Missouri on 5 March 1946. The map of Europe was being redrawn after the war, with the eastern side of the continent now under the control of the Soviet Union. Churchill stated: 'From Stettin in the Baltic to Trieste in the Adriatic, an iron curtain has descended across the Continent.' This memorable description of Soviet might was given a football equivalent by the uncompromising line of committed men defending Bobby Brown's goal who repelled those who tried to break through. There will probably never be a more famous defensive unit in Scottish football.

But this Rangers team boasted a lot more than a formidable defence. The maverick skills of Gillick had been missing for the Old Firm clash, but he was back in his usual place in time for the Glasgow Cup Final in late October. Third Lanark were the opposition and they were swept aside 4-1 with comeback man Gillick scoring one of the goals and adding yet another medal to his collection.

By then, Falkirk had shocked Rangers in the semi-finals of the League Cup, and the league race was already looking like another tight affair with Hibs, who were matching the Rangers results stride for stride. As the season reached the traditional festive programme, Gillick was facing up to the inevitable tragic loss of his daughter, Isobel, but he still managed to produce magic on the pitch. Just as in the previous Christmas period, he hit a spell of goalscoring form. He hit the Aberdeen net twice in a commanding 4-0 Ibrox win before grabbing the only goal of a nervy victory at Third Lanark in the last match before Christmas Day. He then hit the winner at Firhill in the first game after the festivities, keeping Rangers just in front at the top. It meant he had scored the last Rangers goal of 1946 and the first and last goals of 1947.

January started in triumph, but ended in tragedy. A crowd of 60,000 were at Parkhead on 2 January 1948 to see the traditional Old Firm start to the New Year, the match having been postponed the previous day. Celtic must have wished their pitch remained unplayable, as they were ruthlessly outclassed. The pick of four Rangers goals was the third, which featured wonderful interplay between Gillick and Eddie Rutherford and ended with Gillick drawing the goalkeeper and laying the ball on a plate for his wing companion to roll it into the net. Most of the home fans went home long before the referee ended the contest, 4-0 being somewhat flattering to the men in green.

But by 31 January, Gillick was trudging off the field at Easter Road, a man alone despite the 50,000 crowd. He had insisted on playing in the huge top-of-the-table clash, but the death of little Isobel the previous day had broken his heart and the match passed him by completely. This match was the pivotal day of the league season and a last-minute goal gave Hibs a crucial 1-0 victory. Rangers then went on a dismal run, during which they won just two out of eight matches, and the league title was lost. It was noticeable that during this slump the Gillick goals dried up, no doubt due to events away from the football pitch. His only league goal after the Easter Road defeat came in a surprise 3-2 defeat to Queen of the South at Ibrox.

In February, amid this sad personal period for Gillick, the team travelled to Portugal to take on Benfica in a challenge match. This was well before the days of organised continental competition and Rangers were regarded as a massive attraction by the Portuguese public. Gillick had to overcome his fear of flying to join the travelling party, who were astonished when a crowd of around 5,000 locals were gathered at the airport to greet their famous visitors. The one man they seemed most eager to see was Torry, his name chanted by the crowd as the players passed through the airport.

Although they were Portuguese champions, Benfica were no match for Struth's men, Rangers easing to a comfortable 3-0 win with a double by Duncanson and a strike by Thornton making the difference in front of a massive 60,000 crowd. It was a memorable trip for the players, something very different for them, and a taste of what football would become in the years ahead. It was also particularly memorable for two of Gillick's team-mates.

Benfica officials laid on a luxurious banquet in the evening after the game, with the players treated to the best food and drink. Legendary centre-half Willie Woodburn seemed to especially enjoy the champagne and, after more than a few glasses, he developed the habit of standing up to toast his hosts before every new glass. His regular cry of 'Viva Benfica' would prompt his team-mates to coin a new nickname for him that would stick for the rest of his career. From that night onwards, he would be known as 'Big Ben'.

Meanwhile, Gillick's great friend and right-wing partner Willie Waddell would find a totally different kind of partner on the trip. He was attracted to one of the air hostesses on their flight and Hilda would become Mrs Waddell after they began courting once back home in Scotland. Hilda would become a part of the Gillick family's lives for many years, with Torry enjoying many a bowl of her homemade soup in their many visits to the Waddell home.

Poor league results had left the Scottish Cup as the only major prize available for the season and Rangers were determined to bring the old trophy back to Ibrox for the first time since 1936. Gillick was the only Ibrox player with a winner's medal in the tournament, which saw some more massive attendances. Some 68,000 were at Ibrox to see Partick Thistle beaten in the third round, then an unbelievable 90,000 watched East Fife conquered in the last eight thanks to yet another vital Jimmy Duncanson goal. The draw for the semi-finals pitted Rangers against Hibs.

The match attracted the biggest crowd Rangers have ever played before, an incredible 143,570. The *Glasgow Herald* report of the match mentioned that this enormous figure was bolstered by 'an unusually high number of women'. It didn't speculate on either how the reporter arrived at this conclusion or the reason behind the increase. Gillick and his team-mates knew they faced the biggest challenge in the Scottish game, with Hibs having scored in every match they had played that season. It was a match Rangers won thanks to a moment of fortune and then an hour of sheer hard work.

After half an hour, the Hibs stand-in goalkeeper George Farm dropped a Willie Waddell cross at the feet of Willie Thornton. The ball was in the Hibs net a second later. Hibs had an hour to get back in the match and they bombarded the Rangers defence, with the men in blue now straining every sinew to repel the most formidable attacking force in the land. Inside-forwards Gillick and Duncanson dropped deeper to provide extra cover for the beleaguered rearguard, with Gillick and his team-mates exhausted but triumphant when the final whistle blew. Morton shocked Celtic in the other semi-final, played before more than 80,000 at Ibrox that same afternoon, meaning around 225,000 people attended the two ties in the same city at the same time. Now it was the men from Greenock who stood between Gillick and a second Scottish Cup Final victory.

Another huge crowd packed into the national stadium on 17 April for the final, with more than 131,000 there to witness a tense affair. Despite Morton being close to the relegation places in the league, they proved to be stubborn and skilful opponents and they came close to causing a similar upset to 26 years earlier when the Greenock side lifted the trophy for the only time in their history after a shock 1-0 win over Struth's men. On a blustery afternoon that made football difficult, Rangers struggled without both of their regular wingers, with both Willie Waddell and Jimmy Caskie unavailable. They also got off the worst possible start when the fierce crosswind deceived goalkeeper Bobby Brown and he allowed a 40-yard free kick by Morton skipper Jimmy Whyte to sail over him into the net.

This gave the underdogs great heart but, just ten minutes later, Gillick made his first meaningful contribution to the final. A cross was nodded down into his path by Willie Thornton and the man who had scored the first-ever League Cup Final goal the previous year smashed it home to register the first Scottish Cup Final goal for Rangers in the post-war era. There were no goals in the remaining 78 minutes of regulation time, nor in 30 additional minutes. That meant a replay, with Rangers perhaps feeling happier at the prospect than the Morton players, who felt they had probably done enough to have won the cup at the first time of asking.

Struth was unhappy with the performance and made one change to the attack for the rematch four days later. It meant something of a reshuffle, with centre-forward Billy Williamson replacing inside-forward Willie Findlay. It meant Willie Thornton moving to inside-right, Jimmy Duncanson switching to inside-left and the versatile Gillick switching across to the left-wing berth he had occupied 13 years earlier when he last played in a Scottish Cup Final win. No longer with the energy of that 1935 teenager, this represented a challenge to the fitness and running power of the wilier but less explosive Gillick of 1948.

In truth, he found it hard to make any great impression on an impressive Morton defence, who kept the Rangers attack quiet for 117 minutes. Then, just as the 133,750 midweek crowd were expecting another replay, the cup was won. The goalscoring hero was the man called into the team, Billy Williamson. His unstoppable header finished off a sweeping Rangers move, the first Scottish Cup appearance in his entire career given a fairytale ending. For Gillick, it meant a year that started in the most terrible of family tragedies had now produced another record-breaking career highlight. He became the first, and only, player to win the Scottish Cup both before and after the war.

Gillick also added another Charity Cup success to his honours list when Celtic were vanquished in the May final with that man Williamson again opening the scoring. But the end of the 1947/48 season also marked the end of Gillick as an automatic choice in the Rangers team. Now aged 32, he would find himself spending the remainder of his second Ibrox stint as an important member of the squad but one who started fewer matches than he had been accustomed to. Yet that didn't mean he stopped making history.

Gillick didn't feature in the opening fixture of 1948/49 against Motherwell; the inside-right position was filled by Willie Findlay in a match remembered for Willie Woodburn being sent off the first time in his career. Four days later, Falkirk were the season's first visitors to Ibrox, with Gillick restored to the starting XI. Midway through the second half, the visitors enjoyed a 3-1 lead and the 40,000 Ibrox crowd were decidedly unhappy. Then, after Willie Findlay had given Rangers a lifeline, the returning Gillick showed his manager what he had been missing. In the closing stages, he twice scored past Jerry Dawson in the Falkirk goal to drag Rangers to an unlikely 4-3 win and rob his old friend and team-mate Dawson of a memorable return to the stadium he had called home for so long.

A few days later, Gillick started what would be his last Old Firm league match. Fittingly, it was a winning farewell to the fixture, an early Findlay goal enough to earn the points at Parkhead in a match which saw Celtic miss a penalty and pass up a chance to equalise. It would be November before Gillick added to his two strikes against Falkirk, scoring in successive appearances that month against Hibs and St Mirren, helping Rangers step up their annual assault on the league title. However, the game against St Mirren saw Gillick pick up a nasty injury that kept him sidelined for several weeks and, after playing in seven of the first nine league matches of the campaign, he would only start one more league game all season.

That start came at Cathkin Park in a defeat to Third Lanark in mid-January 1949, a result that left Rangers trailing league leaders Dundee by three points. The returning Gillick could hardly have been blamed for the loss, however. He created the Rangers goal for Willie Thornton with a clever headed pass and one Monday morning match report stated: 'Gillick is still the master of the long accurate pass to his winger.' Unfortunately, he was back on the treatment table again after this one fleeting appearance and was only to be chosen once more before the season ended. But what an appearance it was.

Willie Paton had taken over ownership of the inside-right position and, even when Gillick regained fitness, the manager stuck with a winning team. Rangers had started an impressive run of wins and, on 12 March, they were to face Second Division team Raith Rovers in the first domestic final of the season, the League Cup. Rangers were also in the semi-final of the Scottish Cup, a competition for which they were now hot favourites, and their recent form had propelled them into contention in the title race, just behind leaders Dundee. There was a blow in the build-up to the big League Cup Final, with star winger Willie Waddell suffering a muscle injury in a convincing Scottish Cup quarter-final win over Partick Thistle seven days earlier. When Waddell was ruled out, Struth turned to Gillick.

With the passing of time and only one first-team appearance in the previous four months, the veteran Gillick was seriously short of match fitness, and soon after kick-off in the Hampden showpiece in front of nearly 60,000 fans it became obvious he was struggling with the pace of the game. In the *Glasgow Herald* match report, the writer was somewhat scathing of Gillick's efforts, albeit also paying tribute to the player overall. He wrote: 'Gillick was an unexpected deputy at outside-right and his nonchalant meandering was in complete contrast to his former partner's dash and daring. His disinclination to exert himself caused several ripples of amusement among the crowd.' The writer did qualify this criticism by adding: 'I, for one, will remember the Gillick of a year or two ago rather than this caricature of a great player.' Yet, for all the writer's criticisms, it was a moment of Gillick magic that swung the match decisively in Rangers' favour. Rovers had dominated the first half and Rangers had goalkeeper Bobby Brown to thank for a goalless 45 minutes. Many in the crowd were wondering if they were set to witness an historic cup final upset, but within a minute of the restart those thoughts were swept away. Centre-forward Thornton gained possession and took the ball out wide, pulling the Rovers centre-half out of position. Gillick's legs might have no longer been at their fastest, but his football brain was still razor sharp. He immediately saw the possibilities, raced into the gap in the middle and then headed the ball powerfully into the net when Thornton delivered the perfect cross.

Gillick had now played in two League Cup finals and had opened the scoring in both. And he was collecting a second winner's medal after a second goal, scored by Willie Paton, settled the contest and Rangers eased to yet another glory day. That glory would just be the beginning, as Gillick watched his colleagues sweep to the first Treble in Scottish football when they added the Scottish Cup and the league title. Gillick didn't feature again after that first cup triumph of the season, but he enjoyed the celebrations as much as any of the regular starters. The league celebrations were probably staged as much in shock as delight, with Dundee losing 4-1 at Falkirk on the last day when needing only a point to take the flag. Rangers ruthlessly took advantage, a Willie Thornton hat-trick in a 4-1 win at Albion Rovers meaning his goalscoring treble had clinched a trophy treble.

In 1949/50, Rangers successfully defended two of their three pieces of silverware. The league title was retained, but Gillick was now a reserve. Even playing for the second string, he still managed to make the newspapers. In a fiery clash at Palmerston Park against Queen of the South's reserves, the veteran Gillick and his young team-mate Johnny Hubbard both ended up being reported to the SFA for incidents during the match. Hubbard, in his first season at the club after joining in the summer from South African football, was sent off by referee William Harvie of Dalry for the innocuous offence of throwing the ball away when a throw-in decision went against him and he was barracked by the spectators in the vicinity. It was later discovered that Hubbard had been the subject of racial abuse, surely one of the earliest instances of a Rangers player being subjected to this vile treatment. The referee also booked Gillick for a bad-tempered clash with a home defender, the behaviour of both players going into the official's report to the top brass. It's likely that Gillick was far more upset at losing the match 3-0 than any possible reprimand from the authorities.

In the first team, he made just two league starts and collected win bonuses in victories over Aberdeen in October and St Mirren in November. But, by then, he had added another medal to his collection, and his last trophy win as a Rangers player, in October 1949, was the same as his first trophy win back in October 1933. He played in a Glasgow Cup Final win against Clyde.

Unlike 16 years earlier, this final needed a replay before Gillick could raise the beautiful old trophy aloft. And those at the blue end in a 40,000 crowd at Hampden gave him an extra cheer, as the rarely-seen forward proved to be the matchwinner. Clyde were just ten minutes from glory, holding on to a 1-0 lead with time ticking away. As in his League Cup Final performance earlier in the year, one match report mentioned Gillick's approach to the game. The writer remarked that he 'now obviously has to conserve his energy'. In the 80th minute, however, the Rangers supporters were delighted with this strategy. Willie Waddell found Billy Williamson, who played a clever pass into the Clyde penalty box. Gillick, alert as ever, suddenly showed great speed as he raced away from his marker to get there first and rifle the ball home.

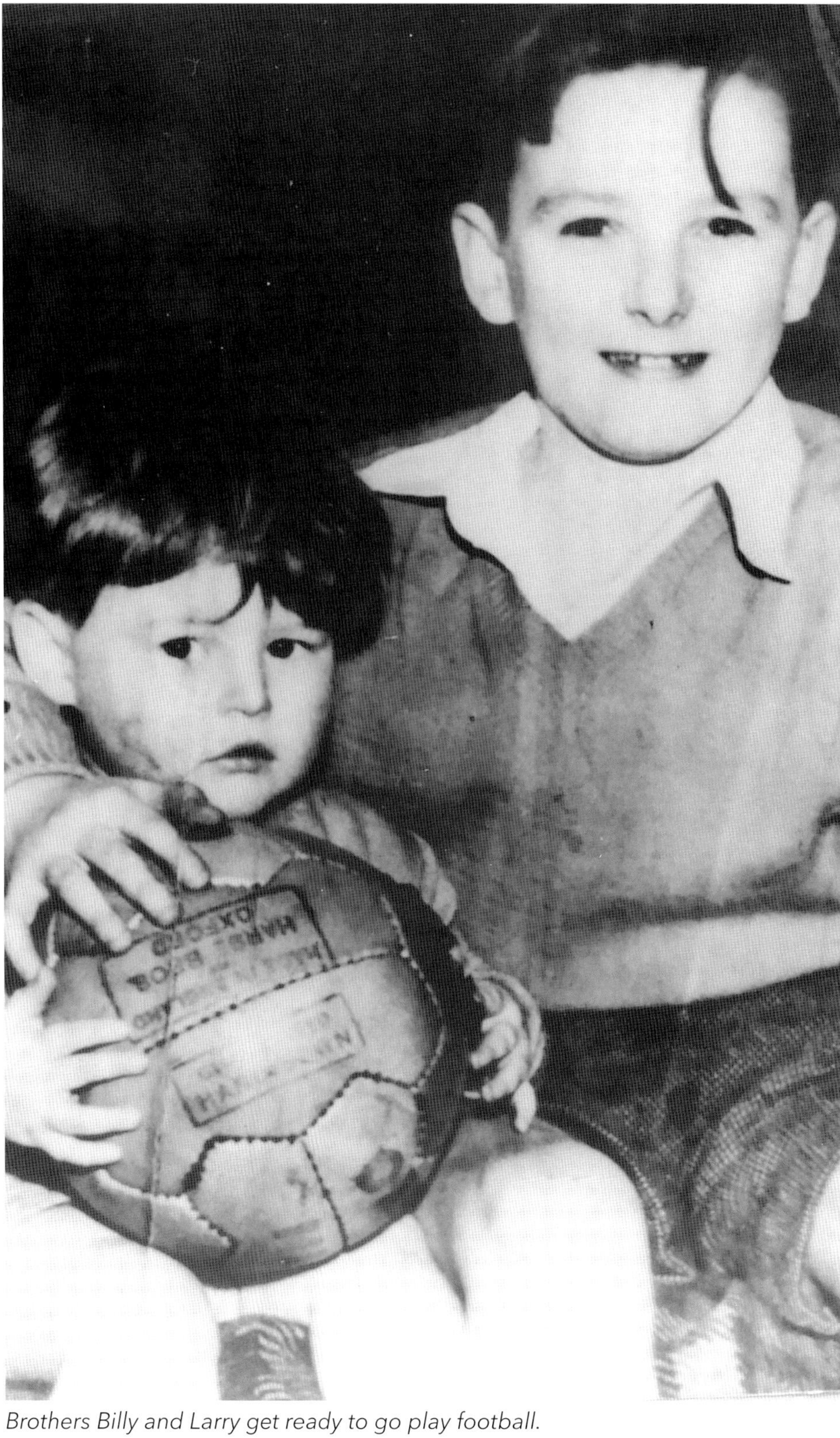

Brothers Billy and Larry get ready to go play football.

Mr and Mrs Gillick, Mr and Mrs Sammy Cox, and Willie Thornton pictured at a wedding.

Rangers' legendary manager Bill Struth with his 'boys' and their wives in the late 1940s.

Torry Gillick, retired footballer and businessman.

Molly and Torry take to the dancefloor at their silver wedding celebration in 1960.

Torry teaches the art of fishing to son Larry.

A happy Torry Gillick after a successful day fishing.

Torry poses with his new motoring pride and joy.

Torry, in fetching headgear, with good friend Norman Macaskill fishing on Loch Duich.

Evidence of success at another sporting love. Two trophies won by the Gillick greyhounds.

Torry with Molly's daughter Jacqueline, his youngest granddaughter.

Granddaughters Esther, Laura, Gillian and Hilary, the daughters of son Billy.

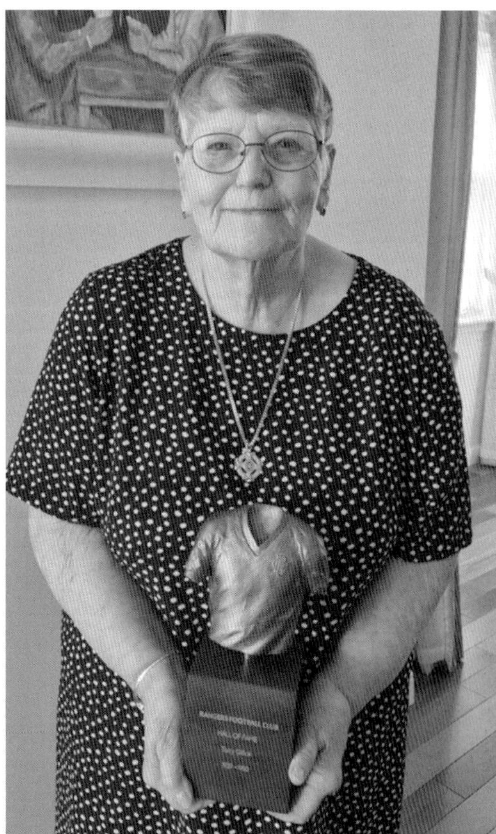

Daughter Molly proudly shows her late father's Rangers FC Hall of Fame trophy in March 2024.

Then with just seven minutes left of an extra half-hour, Gillick completed a memorable double. This time Waddell supplied the through ball, Gillick's vision gave him a yard start on the surrounding defenders and he had the ball past Clyde goalkeeper Charlie Thomson before any Clyde player could react. It ended 2-1, with the *Glasgow Herald* headline summing up the match. 'Waddell-Gillick Triumph' reminded the football public of the great partnership had had one last silver swansong.

Top footballers in the 1940s were not paid anything like the massive wages their modern counterparts enjoy in comparison to the average earnings in the country. With his love of a bet on the greyhounds, and a young family to support, Gillick found ways to supplement his income. By 1949, this had included putting his name on collectable football cards, but a few years earlier another of his money-making ventures had landed him in hot water with the law. He and a friend, David Jack, bought hens and jointly owned a hen run which allowed the pair to sell eggs to the locals at a time of food rationing. One day, another local owner informed the police that two of his birds had gone missing. When the local area was searched, the missing hens were found in the Gillick and Jack henhouse. Despite the pair claiming that the birds must have wandered into their run and they had no knowledge of where they had come from, both men were fined £5 after being found guilty of resetting stolen goods!

Another Gillick story centred around creatures with scales rather than feathers. Towards the end of his Ibrox career, Rangers travelled north for a fixture at Aberdeen, with Gillick not in the travelling party. One of the squad who did go to Pittodrie was centre-forward Billy Williamson. He and his team-mates were on their way north when a delivery of live fish arrived at the stadium for him, a gift from a friend for a garden pond Williamson had recently installed at his home. The delivery was noticed by a certain Torry Gillick.

Williamson found out about the fish waiting for his collection and made his way to Ibrox on the day after the Aberdeen match. The sight greeting him in the dressing room was one he still laughed about decades later. In the home dressing room, the players' communal bath had been filled with water and there were the fish swimming around happily. Beside the bath sat his friend Torry, who had attached string and a homemade hook to a corner flag, and was sitting patiently waiting for a bite! It isn't known if he actually caught any of them.

As the 1949/50 season concluded, there would be one last Gillick masterpiece for the football public to enjoy. The Charity Cup Final in May was the traditional finale to the Glasgow football season and it would be contested by the Old Firm. A crowd of 81,000 were at Hampden, some of them possibly there to get a glimpse of a star of the silver screen who was in Glasgow promoting his latest film. Singer and actor Danny Kaye, one of the most famous faces in Hollywood and star of films such as *The Secret Life of Walter Mitty*, was presented to the teams prior to kick-off and watched the match from the stand.

He saw an unusual Rangers line-up, with stars such as Waddell, Young and McColl all missing and the rarely seen John Lindsay, Adam Little and young Johnny Hubbard all lining up alongside Gillick. In the first half, this untried XI struggled badly, with the ageing Gillick attracting derision for what appeared to some fans as a lack of effort. One particularly brutal match report described his performance in the opening half as 'a token appearance'. In truth, he was likely just struggling with the speed of the game. When Celtic forward John McPhail scored two quick goals just after the break he completed a hat-trick and Rangers were 3-0 adrift. A hammering looked on the cards. Then, as the match started to slow from its frantic pace, Gillick suddenly took centre stage.

After starting at outside right, he switched infield and immediately caused havoc. In the 66th minute, he came close with a shot that fizzed just past. Then, a minute later, Rangers pulled a goal back when Gillick burst clear of the Celtic defence to shoot home. He then twice came close to creating a goal for Thornton, the centre-forward suddenly 'revelling in the confusion Gillick's accurate passing and astute positioning was causing', according to the *Glasgow Herald*. Thornton did get on the scoresheet with 12 minutes remaining and Celtic were now grimly hanging on. But they survived, Gillick running out of steam as the game reached the final minutes, that same report stating that 'this Gillick-inspired spell did not last … age finally gave way to youth'.

Gillick may have bowed out of Ibrox in defeat, but he had reminded everyone present of the natural talent and football brain that would be sorely missed. He left the club that summer at the age of 34. He had enjoyed a Rangers career spanning 17 years across two spells, with 206 goals in 387 competitive appearances. And to give that magnificent career some symmetry, both the first and the 206th goals he scored for Rangers came in cup matches against Celtic.

There was one last disagreement with manager Struth, as Gillick felt aggrieved he didn't receive bonus payments for the club's successful season. With Rangers insisting he hadn't made sufficient appearances in 1949/50 to merit inclusion in the bonus pool, the player felt he had no option but to raise the matter in court. So, just days after his Rangers playing career ended, he raised a legal action against the club for unpaid wages of £70 via his lawyer Mr A. Cruikshank. Happily, the matter never reached court, with the parties agreeing a settlement a few months later. This disagreement had no impact on his relationship with his former boss, or with the club itself; Gillick would always be given the warmest of welcomes whenever he returned to the stadium in the future.

If proof was ever needed of the bond that existed between the great Ibrox disciplinarian and his maverick player, it came a few years later after the death of Struth at the age of 81. His passing was marked by the club with a special edition of the *Rangers Review* in December 1956, a bimonthly publication that was extremely popular with supporters at the time. Several ex-players were featured, paying tribute to the man who had presided over a trophy-winning dynasty. They included Arthur Dixon, Tommy Muirhead, Willie Waddell and, of course, Torry Gillick. The *Review* writer appeared to give a slight nod to the past disputes between manager and player by describing Torry as one of Struth's 'controversial' players.

Gillick revealed that he had turned down the chance to stay on at the club and work under Struth, an offer which would never have been made had Struth had the slightest doubt over his commitment to the Ibrox cause. Gillick said, 'I was offered a job in Mr Struth's office at Ibrox. He wanted me to learn the administrative side to the game – for later.' The exact 'later' role the wily old schemer had in mind wasn't revealed and, despite Gillick's future business success, it was something he still mulled over six years after his final departure from Ibrox as an employee of Rangers. 'Like a fool, I refused,' said Gillick, displaying an unusual sense of regret. 'He knew what he was talking about. I know that now.' Torry had decided when leaving Rangers in 1950 that it was time to build a new life for himself and his family. It was a future that it seemed would now be away from the world of football.

CHAPTER 9
LIFE AFTER IBROX

AFTER GILLICK'S unforgettable swansong in front of Hollywood royalty, he had to face up to life away from his beloved Ibrox. He had now turned 34 and, although he had shown that he hadn't lost his wonderful football brain or his ability to produce moments of brilliance, the fact was his legs no longer had 90 minutes in them for top-level football.

He had already started to try to earn money outside of his Ibrox wages, agreeing to put his name to a series of playing cards in 1948 entitled 'Torry Gillick's Internationals', a series of collectable cards that each featured a cartoon-style illustration of a famous British international footballer on the front with a short biography of the player on the reverse. The manufacturer of these, S&B Products of Glasgow, presumably paid Torry for the use of his name, which seemed to be as far as his actual input into the cards extended. Several of his Rangers team-mates were featured in the collection, although there was no card featuring Torry himself. This was likely due to him not being a post-war international.

Footballer salaries were nothing like the enormous sums that modern players at big clubs can expect, so the family now needed income from elsewhere. Both Torry and Molly set up businesses, with the scrap metal and haulage business T. and M. Gillick & Sons becoming Torry's company. The premises were in the Baillieston area of the city, the yard built on an area of ground Torry had bought a few years earlier. The business would prove to be a highly successful one. Meanwhile, Molly decided to utilise her hairdressing skills to start her own business, opening a salon in Hillfoot, Bearsden called Mary Gillick, Hairdressers. This also proved to be profitable, with daughter Molly later joining her mother as a hair stylist.

But Torry still had the football bug and, in August 1951, he was asked by his old Rangers captain Davie Meiklejohn to consider a return to the game after a year away. The legendary Ibrox defender was now manager of Partick Thistle and he thought the wily old head of Gillick could be an asset to the team when combined with younger legs around him. Torry had his doubts but, such was his massive admiration for Meiklejohn, he decided to come out of retirement and try to live up to the faith his old skipper obviously had in him.

He signed on at Firhill on Friday, 10 August and was deemed fit enough to be given a debut for the Maryhill men a fortnight later in a League Cup match against the formidable Hibernian team of the time at Easter Road. Despite the loss of an early goal, Gillick helped his side to a 1-1 interval score. In the second half, however, he struggled badly as the fitter Hibs defenders took charge and he was powerless to prevent a painful 5-1 loss that proved decisive in Thistle failing to qualify for the latter stages.

After appearing in two more League Cup matches, he was out of the team again and, due to a combination of his declining fitness, injuries, poor form and Thistle having a team who finished in the top six, Gillick was then an infrequent sight in the Partick colours. He started just ten matches for the manager he so admired and scored just the one goal. That goal was the highlight of his best display of the season when Thistle visited Tynecastle in February to face a Hearts side who had been unbeaten at home all season. The *Glasgow Herald* described his performance that Wednesday night as 'a splendid demonstration of effective football with the minimum expense of energy'. This demonstration included a thumping first-half equaliser in a match Thistle won 2-1.

But, just a month later, he donned the Thistle strip for the final time, his last match perhaps fittingly being against his hometown club, Airdrie. It ended 2-2, Gillick again struggling with the pace of the match against opponents he would have dominated in his prime. He knew, and Meiklejohn knew, that Father Time had caught up with him and he called it a day. Tributes poured in from the world of Scottish football as a glittering career ended. One tribute that Gillick himself was particularly proud of came from a player who plied his trade on the other side of the city. Celtic's Charlie Tully stated in an interview in the *Sunday Mail* that Gillick had been 'the greatest inside-forward I have ever seen' and that 'now, there was a man who had such a football brain'. Tully had signed for Celtic in 1948, so had only played against the veteran version of Gillick, which made his compliment all the greater.

Torry's scrap metal business was beginning to gain a reputation for reliability and cost effectiveness and his hard work was rewarded when the company won a contract to remove scrap from the site of the future Dounreay nuclear factory in Caithness. It was a massive project that took many years to complete and it allowed Torry to give seasonal work to a couple of the Macaskill brothers to help them supplement their income, as their work opportunites in Dornie were limited in the winter. He would continue to help them out over the coming years, the brothers spending time down in Glasgow when based out of the main yard. Roddy Macaskill became something of a hit with the local ladies due to his preference for wearing a kilt in any weather!

In May 1953, Gillick agreed to put his name to a weekly column in the *Glasgow Daily News* to supplement his income. Torry himself did little of the actual writing; the arrangement was more that he gave his opinions on the burning issues in Scottish football and a ghostwriter produced the articles. He also briefly entered the licensing trade when he bought the Brandon public house at 41 Brandon Street in the Dennistoun area of the city. Despite the Brandon being successful, the virtually teetotal Torry decided the pub game wasn't for him and he gave up the licence and sold the premises in March 1955 to concentrate on his haulage business.

As the family businesses continued to prosper, it allowed the Gillicks to indulge in several of their passions in their spare time. They bought a caravan, which became their base for countless holidays in the north-west of the country, breaks that invariably included plenty of time in Dornie. To pass the time when the weather kept them inside, Torry would bring along his favourite board game, Scrabble. Molly and the children were to find out that it wasn't just on the football pitch that he had a burning desire to win. He developed a habit of using what he described as 'good old Scots words' whenever he was stuck, with these words invariably not to be found in any dictionary. Torry's razor-sharp wit even had an answer to any challenge to the validity of words like 'braw' or 'lang'. He would simply say: 'We need a Scottish dictionary, not an English one!' The house in Bearsden was getting a bit small for the family, with Billy, Molly and Larry growing fast, and, when Tommy Muirhead decided he would retire to Helensburgh, he sold his large bungalow to the Gillicks. It was a house move of virtually no distance at all, but one that pleased the whole family as it allowed them extra space as well as meaning they stayed close to so many friends.

Dornie became the place the couple wanted to spend as much time as they could. As well as the Macaskills, they met several other families who became great friends and remained an important part of the Gillicks' lives for decades to come. Among these were Harry and Mina Finlay, also business people who ran a company in Ardelve, a small village on Loch Alsh just a mile from Dornie. They became regular visitors to the Gillick family home at New Year, as well as spending time with them in the Highlands.

Another family who grew close to them were William and Pat Gordon. William was affectionally known as 'Ginger' and shared Torry's passion for fishing, meaning they spent many an hour together on the riverbank. The Gordons' nephew, Kenny, would eventually become a relative, marrying the Gillicks' granddaughter, Jacqueline, many years after Torry's death.

It wasn't just fishing holidays in the north of Scotland that Torry came to enjoy. His love of racing saw him invest in both greyhounds and horses as an owner. He had an interest in several racehorses stabled by trainer Larry Keating in County Tipperary, Ireland. This meant he would take the occasional trip across the water to visit the yard in Rocklow Road, Fethard to see for himself how his prize assets were faring. These trips were made by plane, something Torry hated due to his lifelong fear of flying.

In one memorable visit, he was accompanied by young Molly and the weather took a severe turn for the worse just before the flight home. Torry decided to book an earlier flight back to avoid the storm and they ended up on a plane which had started off in the Holy Land. When they boarded the flight, many of the seats were filled with the members of various religions, including several nuns. Despite his fear of flying, this looked like a good omen to Torry, who declared that there would no way this flight could get into trouble with God looking after it!

Greyhounds had always been a particular interest for him; he had been a well-known face at the local dog tracks since before his marriage. Now he would occasionally be in the owners enclosure, with one dog proving especially successful for him. As with his horses, there was an Irish connection, as Skibbereen Border was named after a town in County Cork. Racing dogs weren't the only kind that he enjoyed; the Gillicks had several pet dogs over the years. The favourite of all was Torry's final pet, Robin, a faithful friend and companion who featured in a favourite family photograph with his master.

Along with flying, Torry's other phobia was being recognised and having the attention of fans and wellwishers while spending time with his family. Being a successful footballer with the biggest team in the country would inevitably lead to requests for autographs and people wanting to reminisce with him about games and goals from his past. Whenever he took the family out, whether simply to the local shops or further afield to a beach or a holiday spot, he would warn the children not to admit who they were. His favourite response to the much-repeated query 'are you Torry Gillick?' was to deny he even knew who that was and had no great interest in football. With his sense of mischief, he would sometimes follow it up by asking whether this guy Gillick was any good, intrigued to see what answer he got. No doubt that depended on whatever team the admirer supported.

This approach sometimes worked, but did occasionally backfire. One night he took the family to a Glasgow theatre to see a show by the popular comedian Lex McLean, a man almost as well known for his love of Rangers as his jokes. After Torry telling the gentleman sitting beside him that he was mistaken and that he didn't know who Torry Gillick was, he was mortified when McLean stopped his show, had the spotlight shone on Torry in the audience and proceeded to tell the audience that one of his Rangers heroes was amongst them!

His name was still revered at Ibrox, despite it now being almost a decade since he had entertained the crowds with his football skills. And, although the 1950s were a relatively successful decade for the club, there were many who pined for another inside-right of similar craft and vision in the blue jersey. Those who reminisced about Torry's talents were not confined to the terraces of Ibrox stadium. In October 1958, journalist Ian Peebles covered the Ibrox clash between Rangers and Raith Rovers for the *Evening News*. The match ended in a highly entertaining 4-4 draw, but the headline wasn't about the feast of goals the 30,000 crowd had watched.

His report was entitled 'Shades of Gillick', a reference to the wonderful display of vision and passing from the recent Rangers recruit from Airdrie, Ian McMillan. Not only did McMillan pull the strings in the middle that day, he also scored two excellent goals. Peebles wrote: 'What a joy to watch McMillan killing that ball and dispatching it with deadly accuracy. They haven't cheered this kind of stuff at Ibrox since Torry Gillick left.' Considering Rangers had already won three league titles in the post-Gillick era, it showed what a standout performer he must have been. The man himself was certainly proud as punch when he found out about the article.

In November 1959, Torry would lose his beloved mother, Isabella, at the age of 67. She was interred alongside husband, Lawrence, and her tragic little granddaughter, Isabel, at Old Monklands. This meant the old family home in Gartness now housed Torry's younger sister, Kate, her husband, Willie, and their daughter, who was also called Isabel.

By the early 1960s, there was only Larry left at home, with both the other children having flown the nest. Torry felt it was time to go back home and the couple bought a plot of land in the area of Wester Moffat, just outside Airdrie and close to Gartness. The house they had built there was to be the final family home Torry and Molly would share.

At this time, Larry was looking like he might follow in his father's footsteps. He was attracting plenty of attention as a young amateur footballer and he even featured in an article in the *Evening Times* which proclaimed another Gillick may be about to take the football world by storm. Despite his obvious talent, he joined the ranks of the countless other young footballers whose dreams never materialised and he ended up going down a totally different career path.

The trips north to Dornie continued, of course. And, as well as enjoying plenty of days and nights with the Macaskills on the shores of the local lochs, Torry had struck up a friendship with another local who enjoyed salmon fishing. John Farquar Munro was a real character and the virtually teetotal Torry watched him sink a few drams as they tried to entice the fish to bite. A small sherry at New Year was as much alcohol as Torry ever wanted; the fresh air, a fishing rod in one hand and a Capstan cigarette or a Tom Thumb cigar in the other gave him all the pleasure he needed.

Torry and John shared another passion, a love of quality motor cars and, when Torry turned up in Dornie driving his prize Rover 90, John was the happiest man in the district when he was allowed to take it for a spin. In his later years, John found fame of his own when he was elected MSP for the constituency of Ross, Skye and Inverness West after standing for the Liberal Democrats in the first election for the new Scottish parliament in 1999. He would own several impressive motor cars of his own before he passed away in 2014.

Torry obviously retained his keen interest in football and took under his wing a local boy called Alex Forsyth. Young Alex grew up in Baillieston and Gillick would take the youngster for walks where he taught him how to play the game, kicking rubber balls and tin cans using his right and left foot. The lessons obviously paid off, Forsyth going on to star for Partick Thistle and Manchester United, while winning ten Scotland caps. In August 1978, he left Old Trafford to join Rangers, initially on a loan deal. When interviewed about his move to the Scottish champions, Forsyth spoke warmly about the influence the former Ibrox idol had been, saying Gillick's unique lessons were not so good for his shoes but perfect for teaching a kid how to control a ball with both feet.

As the 1960s ended, the Gillicks were now proud grandparents several times over. Billy and his wife, Esther, had four children, all of them girls. Esther, Hilary, Gillian and Laura were regular visitors to Wester Moffat where they were, of course, spoiled rotten. The children were also treated to trips north to the caravan, enjoying card games when the weather didn't allow them out in the fresh air. Molly's first marriage also produced a daughter, little Jacqueline making it five girls out of five, prompting their doting Papa to declare that 'we might never have a football team so we'll just need to have a hockey team instead'.

In late 1971, while working at the haulage yard in Ballieston, Torry had a fall from a roof after going up there to look at a repair it needed. His injuries were minor; at least it seemed this way at the time. He did bump his head, but nothing seemed seriously amiss and the incident was soon virtually forgotten. Unknown to some in the family, he complained of headaches and dizziness occasionally over the following days and, despite him brushing this off, it was probably the first signs of something being badly wrong.

A few weeks later, after reporting the dizziness and headaches to a doctor he was admitted to the Royal Infirmary in Glasgow for tests. On his release, he was told to rest and not exert himself too much. A *Rangers News* report in early December stated that Gillick was 'back home after a recent spell in hospital'. It described him as 'progressing well'. Sadly, that prognosis was to prove overly optimistic.

Wife Molly's birthday was coming up on 15 December, a day of the year that Torry always made sure was special. As was his custom, he treated her to a day in the city centre the day before her big day, which always included him buying her a birthday gift in Fraser's department store as well as getting a few last-minute presents for the children and grandchildren from Santa. Molly chose a dress, the plan being that she would wear it the following evening at her birthday dinner.

Son Larry and young granddaughter Jacqueline were both in the house next morning when it was time to sing 'Happy Birthday', after which Torry went to the bathroom to shave and get ready for the birthday festivities ahead. It would be a celebration that never happened. While in the bathroom, Torry collapsed. He had suffered a devastating brain aneurism and was unconscious when the family rushed in after hearing him fall to the floor.

Larry was the first to find him and it was obvious straight away that this was a dire emergency. An ambulance quickly arrived and Larry and his mother accompanied Torry as the ambulance sped off to the Royal Infirmary, the rest of the family following on as quickly as they could. Despite the best efforts of the doctors, they had no chance of saving him and Torry Gillick died aged just 55. In a sad coincidence, it was the same age his father had been when he passed away.

Needless to say, the entire family was in shock, no one more than his soul mate, Molly. It was a birthday she would always remember for all the wrong reasons; the dress her husband had bought her the previous day would now forever be left unworn.

15 December 1971 would go down in Rangers club history as a particularly sad day, as there was a second legendary former player who passed away that same date. 'Wee Blue Devil' Alan Morton, whose incredible Ibrox playing career ended just before Torry had signed from Petershill in 1933 and who was by then a director of the club, died at the age of 78.

Tributes poured in from across the football world for the sudden loss of Torry Gillick, with the double Rangers heartache the headline news in many morning papers. Perhaps the most poignant tribute came from his old Rangers team-mate and the Rangers manager of the time, Willie Waddell. Writing in the club's newspaper, the *Rangers News*, Waddell penned a touching article entitled 'Torry Gillick, My Friend' in which he told of the many precious times he and his wife, Hilda, had shared with Torry and Molly and of the wonderful stories Torry could tell of his life on and off the pitch. He described the pair's long-lasting relationship, which the public only saw in the blue of Rangers but that, away from the football pitch, was based on so much laughter and mutual good-natured ribbing. Each man claimed the credit for making the other look good! Waddell also joked about how Torry would particularly enjoy a bowl of Hilda's soup at 2am before deciding it was time to go home.

Waddell paid tribute to the marvellous football ability of the man whose right-wing partnership with him had helped the club to so many great victories and much silverware. 'It was a football treat to play beside him for so many years,' said Waddell. 'If a pass was on, he made the pass.' He added: 'Give him a ball at his feet … and he was in a class of his own. He could size up a situation in a flash and do in one move what others took three to do … Torry was a craftsman. And, like all great craftsmen, he made his job look easy.' Before closing his tribute with how much he would miss his friend, Waddell summed up the ability of Gillick by stating simply: 'Torry was one of the greats.' Then, in a nod to the jocular relationship they had shared, the Ibrox manager added: 'I never expressed that opinion to him, of course, but now I write it without reservation.' On 17 December 1971, the entire Rangers playing squad, management staff and board all attended the funerals of both the legendary stars of the club's past. Torry was buried in the same Old Monklands cemetery as his parents and precious daughter Isabel, while Morton was laid to rest in the nearby New Monklands graveyard. While Rangers had lost two immortal names, the Gillick family were mourning the unexpected loss of a husband, father and papa who meant the world to them all. Life would never be the same again for them.

But Torry Gillick left behind a unique football story, one that remains imprinted on the histories of both Rangers and Scottish football. He was the only player signed twice by Bill Struth. He was the only player to win the Scottish Cup both before and after the Second World War. He scored a hat-trick in the biggest-ever competitive win in an Old Firm match. And he was the first player ever to score in a Scottish League Cup Final. Then, almost a year after his death, he managed to create another record. He became the first Rangers player mentioned in a debate in the House of Commons.

In a heated debate on Northern Ireland on 13 November 1972, Dick Douglas, the Labour MP for Clackmannan and East Stirlingshire, said this in reply to comments made by the Irish Nationalist MP Bernadette Devlin:

'I regret what was said today by the Honourable Lady, the Member for Mid-Ulster. She completely misinterprets the situation as I see it. She talks in class terms, in terms of irreconcilables. I do not know which class she is speaking for, but she certainly does not speak for my class in Northern Ireland. She does not speak for the Protestant workers and I do not believe that she really speaks for the Catholic workers either, because they do not want a challenge to the established order in the way that she sees it. I dislike Tories as well. There is a saying, if I may be colloquial, that the only good Tory was Tory Gillick and he played for Glasgow Rangers. However, although one may dislike people and their policies, one is not bound to oppose them in the way that the Honourable Member for Mid-Ulster gave the impression that she opposes them.'

This is how the quote appeared in Hansard, the official record of the UK Houses of Parliament, with the mis-spelling of his first name reflecting some poetic licence on Douglas's part, but it was an example of how, even after his death, the Gillick name was known all over the country. Decades later, his name is still revered by fans of both Rangers and Everton and he is a massive source of pride to the family he left behind all those years ago.

CHAPTER 10
A PROUD FAMILY

TORRY'S DEATH in 1971 ended his dream of moving north to Dornie to live out his retirement there with Molly. But Molly was determined that she would keep their promise to each other and the following year she sold up and relocated to the place that held so many great memories for her.

She would go on to establish a whole new life there, becoming a much-loved and valued member of the local community for the next 30 years. Her love of home baking came in handy for the countless fetes and events that she helped make a success, with her cakes and scones enjoyed by generations of families. Daughter Molly moved north, too, along with daughter Jacqueline, as three generations slowly came to regard the Highlands as their home.

Molly enjoyed many friendly, and sometimes competitive, poker and whist evenings. Her kindness and community spirit became legendary in the village, Molly often coming to the rescue and offering lifts to youngsters without transport as they walked home. She and her faithful little canine companion, Chico, were a regular sight. Chico certainly enjoyed a life of luxury, Molly ensuring he wanted for nothing. His daily routine included being fed the best cuts of meat and enjoying the luxury of having his fur brushed and a talcum powder 'pampering' to ensure he looked his best.

And whether it was in the car, out in the street or indoors, Molly would thoroughly enjoy telling stories of her life alongside one of the greatest Scottish footballers of his generation and of a life that involved so many great friends in the world of football.

Molly always insisted that her husband would have ideally wanted to be buried in the Highlands, which he wanted to call home. When she passed away in November 2004 at the age of 90, there was no doubt where she would be laid to rest. Her gravestone in Clachan Duich cemetery is quickly found, the massive Rangers FC crest on it a homage to the man she loved and to the club he was so proud to represent.

Granddaughter Jacqueline remains a native of the area to this day, married to the nephew of Pat and 'Ginger' Gordon, who were among the closest of family friends to the Gillicks. Along with her husband, Kenny, and her mother, Molly junior, they make sure the memories of Torry's amazing career live on, with medals, photographs and other treasured memorabilia all on display. Travel a few hours south and the home of the Gillicks's youngest son, Larry, is the same, visitors seeing pictures and clippings from a unique football career as soon as they enter the living room. Meanwhile, in Glasgow, granddaughter Hilary proudly shows off her collection of

Torry memorabilia, which includes medals won at football as well as trophies won as a greyhound owner.

Reasons to be proud of their much-loved father and grandfather continued many years after his death. In 1999, Rangers announced they would be establishing a club Hall of Fame, with chairman Sir David Murray, club historian David Mason and legendary former players John Greig and Sandy Jardine responsible for creating the selection criteria for inductees, as well as choosing an initial group of legends to be honoured in this exclusive club. They agreed on five criteria would-be inductees would be judged on; service to the club, number of games played, honours won with Rangers, international caps won while at Rangers and exceptional ability.

Given these guidelines, it was no surprise that, within a few years of the Hall of Fame's launch, the name of Torry Gillick was added to the list of the most celebrated former Ibrox players. In time, he would be joined by a great many of his team-mates from his first and second spells as a Rangers player. By the summer of 2023, Rangers FC had awarded this ultimate honour to just 100 players, with the recent inductions of Steve Davis, Allan McGregor and James Tavernier completing the century.

All 100 names are displayed on a board at the top of the iconic marble staircase in the main entrance of the Bill Struth main stand at Ibrox. There is also now a club museum, where each player is featured on a striking photographic wall, with visitors able to read about their achievements and even attempt the impossible task of selecting a greatest XI from the 100 names. Torry Gillick is in exalted company, but there is no doubt he belongs among the elite names from more than 150 years of an iconic football club.

But, although he is mainly remembered in Scotland as a Rangers great, there is another historic football club where his name is equally revered. Everton FC also introduced a Hall of Fame in 1999 and among the list of legendary players afforded this highest honour is the name of Torry Gillick.

Unlike the Ibrox version, the Goodison Hall of Fame inducts non-players as well as those who excelled on the pitch, so it has slightly more members than the Rangers equivalent. As of 2023, Gillick had 130 colleagues in Everton's roll of honour. One of them is his great friend Gordon Watson, who was inducted for his lifetime of service to the club, having spent 63 years on the staff at Goodison in various roles that included first-team coach, promotions officer and even matchday barman.

There are several other former Rangers stars alongside him, as well as most of the 1938/39 title winners Gillick played alongside. Among those with an Ibrox connection are Gary Stevens, Trevor Steven, Duncan Ferguson and Andy Gray. But Gillick is one of only two players to have his name in the list of both clubs, the other being winger Alex Scott.

The Gwladys Street Hall of Fame – named after the end of Goodison Park where the most fervent home fans gather – has a short description of Gillick under his name and picture, a description that sums up in a few words why he was so loved and admired by football fans everywhere. It simply reads: 'Torry Gillick, 1935/36 to 1945/46. Simply bamboozled opponents with his magnetic ball control.' Being part of the all-time greats at each club isn't just something that fills the remaining Gillick family with immense pride, it also can have unexpected benefits. In October 2022, Torry's granddaughter, Jacqueline, and her husband, Kenny, were planning a trip to Glasgow as part of their silver wedding celebrations. They decided to book a table at the restaurant inside Ibrox stadium as well as buying match tickets and a tour of the stadium. While on the telephone booking tickets, Jacqueline mentioned how great it would be to be back inside Ibrox, as it was where her papa had been so proud to play his football. This remark kicked off a series of events that left a lifelong memory.

Shortly after hanging up, Jacqueline received a call from Rangers, enquiring who her famous relative was. When she explained her grandfather was Torry Gillick, the club decided that the upcoming tour would be upgraded to a VIP experience. The couple were also invited to the next home match as guests of the club.

On the Friday, a tour guide met them at the main entrance and gave them a guided tour of the magnificent main stand, now named after Torry's former boss Bill Struth. They were shown the trophy room, which still contained some of the trophies her grandfather had won, and the Hall of Fame board he featured on. They walked down the tunnel to stand on the pitch Torry had graced decades before.

The entire day was captured on the club's official television channel, with a nervous Jacqueline interviewed and telling of her immense pride and gratitude. But their VIP experience wasn't yet over.

The following day was matchday and it started with a visit to the famous Blue Room. There they were met by Joe Morrison, the curator of the upcoming Rangers Museum and he had a couple of special items of memorabilia associated with Torry's career. First, the minutes of the board meeting in 1933 that documented his signing from Petershill. Then, a diary which was kept by another member of the club's Hall of Fame, Arthur Dixon, who was the team trainer at the time. In it, he had written out the team lines and scorers of the games the team took part in, including Torry's debut against Partick Thistle. The family were astonished and delighted in equal measure. Morrison was equally delighted to have had the chance to show off these treasures, as he would also reveal that Gillick was the football hero of his Rangers-daft papa.

Club chairman Stewart Robertson also met them and they enjoyed a pre-match meal with him and several other club VIPs before watching from the directors' box as Rangers defeated Aberdeen 4-1, rounding off a day that will never be forgotten. They met such well-known Rangers faces as John Greig, Colin Stein, Archie Knox and lifelong supporter and comedian Andy Cameron. Clips of the visit were released on the Rangers Twitter and YouTube feeds and received tens of thousands of views from across the globe.

There is a reason why Rangers treated the family like club royalty, as that is exactly what Torry Gillick was.

On 31 July 2023, Rangers opened their brand-new club museum, with club legend John Greig performing the ribbon-cutting at the opening ceremony. It has proved to be a hugely popular visitor attraction to fans of the club and, needless to say, there are several reminders of Gillick's Rangers career among the galaxy of exhibits. He is featured in the top row on the Hall of Fame Wall, where faces of all the club legends are included in a wall of individual faces, with visitors able to find out about their Ibrox careers by touching the screens. There are medals and shirts from famous cup finals and other iconic occasions when he played in the team. There is even his passport from the 1930s, which allowed both him and Molly to travel abroad at a time when women didn't need a passport of their own!

We can only wonder what this marvellously unique talent would have made of the modern game, but maybe an interview with the *Evening Times* in 1967 gives a hint of what he would think of 21st century football tactics. He was asked for his thoughts on the game in the 1960s, a period when most older football fans would still claim it was an era of entertainment. Gillick, however, disagreed. Describing the football as 'defensive rubbish', he went on to state: 'I made my name using my brains. I would definitely have refused to play that type of game; it is all drill and no skill. We tried to entertain and score goals at the same time. If we don't get back to that way of thinking, football will die a slow death.' Gillick's achievements made him someone worth listening to. His 206 competitive goals put him in the top ten all-time goalscorers for Rangers and only 39 players in club history to the date of writing have played more competitive matches. His place in Ibrox immortality is secure. His was a career, and a life, that deserves to be remembered. A man who made football fans smile, who created memories on and off the football field and who continues to make his family proud long after he passed away.

In among those great times, there were also sad ones that shaped his life off the pitch. The death of his in-laws so early in his life with Molly was just the first tragedy that was overcome with great courage and character. Poor little Isobel remains in the hearts of her surviving siblings and the uncanny coincidence that saw father Lawrence, sisters Annie and Kate, as well as Torry himself all pass away at the age of just 55 further emphasises the tragedy among the triumphs.

Those tragedies are all part of the tapestry that was the life of Torrance Gillick, a football giant, an entertainer, a unique character and a successful businessman. And, most of all, a family man.

Torry Gillick, 1916–1971.

APPENDIX

TORRY GILLICK CAREER STATISTICS (COMPETITIVE MATCHES)

RANGERS FC 1933–35 & 1940–50		
	GAMES	GOALS
SCOTTISH LEAGUE	104	49
SCOTTISH CUP	16	5
SCOTTISH LEAGUE CUP	20	8
SOUTHERN LEAGUE*	147	86
WARTIME CUPS*	60	38
CHARITY CUP	15	7
GLASGOW CUP	25	13
TOTAL	387	206

EVERTON FC 1935–45		
	GAMES	GOALS
ENGLISH LEAGUE	121	40
FA CUP	12	4
WARTIME COMPETITIONS*	9	4
TOTAL	142	48

AIRDRIEONIANS FC 1940		
	GAMES	GOALS
WESTERN LEAGUE*	6	3
EMERGENCY WAR CUP*	4	1
TOTAL	10	4

PARTICK THISTLE FC 1951–52		
	GAMES	GOALS
SCOTTISH LEAGUE	7	1
SCOTTISH LEAGUE CUP	3	0
TOTAL	10	1

SCOTLAND		
	GAMES	GOALS
FULL INTERNATIONALS	5	3
WARTIME INTERNATIONALS*	3	0
LEAGUE INTERNATIONALS	3	1
TOTAL	11	4

TOTAL SENIOR CAREER	GAMES	GOALS
	560	263

*Wartime matches were in unofficial competitions, meaning these appearances and goals do not always feature in players' career statistics. As they were competitive matches played for nationally recognised trophies and were played in front of the paying public, they are included here.